CYBER VICTIMOLOGY

Cyber Victimology provides a global socio-legal-victimological perspective on victimisation online, written in clear, non-technical terms, and presents practical solutions for the problem.

Halder qualitatively analyses the contemporary dimensions of cyber-crime victimisation, aiming to fill the gap in the existing literature on this topic. A literature review, along with case studies, allows the author to analyse the current situation concerning cyber-crime victimisation. A profile of victims of cyber-crime has been developed based on the characteristics of different groups of victims. As well, new policy guidelines on the basis of UN documents on cyber-crimes and victim justice are proposed to prevent such victimisation and to explore avenues for restitution of justice for cases of cyber-crime victimisation. This book shows how the effects of cyber victimisation in one sector can affect others. This book also examines why perpetrators choose to attack their victim/s in specific ways, which then have a ripple effect, creating greater harm to other members of society in unexpected ways.

This book is suitable for use as a textbook in cyber victimology courses and will also be of great interest to policy makers and activists working in this area.

Debarati Halder received a LLB degree from University of Calcutta, a LLM degree in International and Constitutional Law from University of Madras, a LLM degree in Criminal and Security Law from Parul University, and a PhD (Law) from NLSIU, Bangalore. She is Professor of Law at Parul Institute of Law, Parul University, Gujarat, India.

CYBER VICTIMOLOGY

Decoding Cyber-Crime Victimisation

Debarati Halder

NEW YORK AND LONDON

First published 2022
by Routledge
605 Third Avenue, New York, NY 10158

and by Routledge
2 Park Square, Milton Park, Abingdon, Oxon, OX14 4RN

Routledge is an imprint of the Taylor & Francis Group, an informa business

© 2022 Taylor & Francis

The right of Debarati Halder to be identified as author of this work has been asserted by her in accordance with sections 77 and 78 of the Copyright, Designs and Patents Act 1988.

All rights reserved. No part of this book may be reprinted or reproduced or utilised in any form or by any electronic, mechanical, or other means, now known or hereafter invented, including photocopying and recording, or in any information storage or retrieval system, without permission in writing from the publishers.

Trademark notice: Product or corporate names may be trademarks or registered trademarks, and are used only for identification and explanation without intent to infringe.

Library of Congress Cataloging-in-Publication Data
Names: Halder, Debarati, 1975- author.
Title: Cyber victimology : decoding cyber crime victimization / Debarati Halder.
Description: New York, NY : Routledge, 2022. | Includes bibliographical references and index.
Identifiers: LCCN 2021020202 (print) | LCCN 2021020203 (ebook) | ISBN 9781498784894 (hbk) | ISBN 9781032107523 (pbk) | ISBN 9781315155685 (ebk)
Subjects: LCSH: Computer crimes. | Victims of crimes.
Classification: LCC HV6773 .H34 2022 (print) | LCC HV6773 (ebook) | DDC 362.88–dc23
LC record available at https://lccn.loc.gov/2021020202
LC ebook record available at https://lccn.loc.gov/2021020203

ISBN: 978-1-4987-8489-4 (hbk)
ISBN: 978-1-032-10752-3 (pbk)
ISBN: 978-1-315-15568-5 (ebk)

DOI: 10.4324/9781315155685

Typeset in Bembo
by KnowledgeWorks Global Ltd.

Dedicated to my daughter

CONTENTS

Preface	*ix*
List of Abbreviations	*xiii*
Acknowledgements	*xiv*
About the Author	*xvi*

1 Introduction: From Victimology to Cyber Victimology   1

   1.1   *Background 1*
   1.2   *Why Cyber Victimology? 4*

2 Patterns of Cyber Victimisation and the Role of Victims and Perpetrators   13

   2.1   *General Patterns of Cyber-Crime Victimisation 13*
   2.2   *Profiling Victims of Cyber-Crimes 26*

3 Victims' Rights in Cyberspace   36

   3.1   *Introduction 36*
   3.2   *Freedom of Speech and Expression on the Internet 38*
   3.3   *Right to Privacy 40*
   3.4   *The Right to be Protected Against Online Sexual Offences 43*
   3.5   *Right to Equal Access to Justice and Fair Trial 44*

4 Issues and Challenges in Policing Cyber-Crimes   47

   4.1   *Policing New Patterns of Cyber-Crimes 47*
   4.2   *Jurisdiction as the Biggest Challenge for Policing Cyber-Crimes 52*

5 Assistance for Cyber-Crime Victimisation   57

   5.1   *International Instruments for Victim Assistance and Their Application for Victims of Cyber-Crimes 57*
   5.2   *Victim Assistance from Non-Governmental Stakeholders 63*

viii Contents

5.3 *Victim Assistance from Intermediaries 64*
5.4 *Victim Assistance from the Criminal Justice Machinery 66*

6 Penology for Cyber Victimisation: Criminal Justice and Societal Responses 73

6.1 *The Ever-Expanding Dimension of Penology 73*
6.2 *Critical Analysis of Punishments Prescribed by Different Jurisdictions for Cyber Offences 75*
6.3 *Reformative and Therapeutic Jurisprudential Approaches to Cyber Penology 81*

7 Conclusion 94

Glossary 97
Index 99

PREFACE

Victimology has always attracted me. I have always believed, as several researchers and practitioners have indicated, that the rights of the accused are weighted somewhat more heavily than the rights of the victims. This is inevitable: from time immemorial accused persons have been victimised by those that governed and, to a large extent, by the criminal justice system. When does a person turns into the accused? There are several standards of rights, responsibilities, and limitations around the globe which may categorise a person accused of an offence if the same crosses the said standard. The ancient legal philosophers knew that if a man was not given the right to fair trial, the entire society would fall victim to autocracy and the misuse and abuse of sovereign power; and the cycle of blood feud, hate crimes, and victimisation would continue indefinitely. The ancient Vedic scriptures, and the Greek and Roman scriptures therefore advocated the creation of a body of rights for the accused. The Arthashashtra from the civilisation of ancient India and Hammurabi's Code of ancient Greece were the first codified rules detailing the rights of the accused. Simultaneously, however, these ancient codes also emphasised the rights of the victims. The golden age of victimology in ancient times was a time period that gave a preference to victims' rights. The victim's demand of justice was often reflected in the commands of the king for the restitution of justice, though this does not mean that the accused was not given any rights. Slowly, the criminal justice system began to forget the demands of the original victims. Over time, patterns of crime changed and the State started assuming the position of the main victim in matters of crime, overshadowing the position of the original victim. State-made rules began deciding the fate of the victims whose rights were relegated instead to the sideline as best witnesses. As the state-made rules for deciding the criminality of the perpetrator crystalised, the latter obtained further rights of protection from the atrocities of the State machineries. The correctional administration and a system of bail were introduced and improved. Some categories of perpetrators could be released from the prison systems and returned to society under the surveillance of the State machineries. But the fear victims had of repeated harms or revengeful activities by the perpetrators would remain forever. The criminal justice system, including the policing system, continued to develop yet this system also included corrupt practices. White-collar crimes grew, which caused the criminal justice system to become stricter in enforcement.

By the late 17th and 18th centuries, the evolution of criminology saw more development in the understanding of why people commit crimes. New patterns of criminal activity and criminals

x Preface

became recognised. The criminal justice system started adopting more compassionate approach towards-time offenders, young offenders, and offenders who had broken the laws for their own survival. In the aftermath of World Wars I and II States were recognised as 'victims'. The patterns of crimes further expanded to include several other types of offences, including trafficking. Scientific developments led to the potential for criminal misuse of weapons and technology. Scientific experiments required more 'subjects' for testing and human beings belonging to the lower economic strata, disabled people, and war convicts were designated as the first choice for such experiments. Slowly, the position of victim turned offender started to receive recognition from the criminal justice machinery. There was a gradual shift in the understanding of the causation of crime: it was no longer thought to be 'genetical,' as Lombroso had characterised it. Psycho-sociological reasons for criminality started to gain more acceptance. This in turn slowly led to the rise of in claiming of victims' responsibilities for causing crime victimisation. By the middle of the 19th century victimology became of interest to defense lawyers, who sought to save their clients from conviction of criminal responsibility in the courts. Post-Second World War, international stakeholders advocated charters of human rights, which necessarily included offenders' and victims' rights. But it was not until 1985 that the rights of the victims were codified by the United Nations for the sake of saving human society as a whole from the effects of an imbalance between the rights of the accused, the offenders, and the victims.

After the Second World War, the Cold War began, which involved the use of machines and devices to store data, including military data. The United States and the erstwhile USSR started developing their powers by innovations in computer technology that would help both countries secure their military intelligentsia on the one hand, and empower them to attack any other remote computers to destroy the military and government operations of their enemies, on the other. But behind every successful machine operation, there is a human brain: with the growth of time, computers and cyberspace no longer remained the protected properties of the military or of the governments. Soon, cyberspace was crowded by individual customers and companies making smarter products (including software) to enable every need of modern human life. The developments of cyberspace began to have an impact on real life. I grew up in a transition era. As children, we enjoyed outdoor activities. Our teachers at schools encouraged us to read more books. The smell of new books seemed heavenly to many of us. At home we could afford to have only one colour television set, and some families, including ours, could also afford to have a landline telephone. I saw post offices extremely busy during festivals. Christmas was the busiest season for these offices, as there would be heaps of ragbags full of letters, cards, and gifts that would be dispatched to the recipients. I was born many years after the Soviet Union launched Sputnik into space (1957) and the United States made the first Moon Landing (1969). But children of my generation knew god did not send us pictures of the surface of the moon or how the planet earth looked from space. We knew that there were computers behind all these marvels. We came to know about the existence of handheld mobile phones in the late 1990s. Much to the shock, surprise, and amusement of our grandparents (the majority of whom saw the Second World War, the Pearl Harbor attack, Hiroshima and Nagasaki being destroyed by atomic bombs, and parts of Asia and Africa being freed from European colonialism), these phones did not have permanent wires attached to them. We helped them read the texts that the phones would receive from our relatives and friends staying overseas; later, we would even see them talking to us through computer screens. I grew up as part of a generation that stopped reading paperback porn magazines and instead watched porn video clips—designed to entertain viewers in a maximum time limit of ten minutes—on their own private mobile screens. An enormous business grew up for sharing protected music and movie scenes secretly. The 2001 Twin Tower attack was a momentous event! The world came to know that terrorists could capture and control the an entire aviation system without actually physically hijacking the control rooms at the airports. It was an attack on the computers and computer systems. Since then, there have been several incidences of attacks on protected systems of the government. By the first few years of the millennium, there had been a revolution in the internet and digital communication systems because of the boom in social media companies. Internet penetration into the lives of the general public grew enormously, and there was a boom in the smart phone industry as well. People preferred plastic money, and the banks started to expand their e-services. But this brought one risk after another: bank accounts became targeted by thieves. A large number of people grew their network for illegal profit making. Men and women of all ages are now targets. I now reside in an era where we cannot expect privacy even when we use our private washrooms, a place which, even two decades earlier, was considered to be a very private area in any home. Our children are becoming increasingly addicted to games available in cyberspace. They prefer to see blogs and videos on YouTube and other apps to understand science and solve math problems. By the time I was finishing this manuscript, the entire world went into lockdown due to the Covid-19 pandemic. But we remained connected with each other, *could go* to the office, begin new jobs and witness more money theft, violence, and chaos while being in home quarantine. The internet never went into lockdown. We were able to see the huge emergence of victims of cyber-crimes. Existing laws have been challenged by smart perpetrators almost every second since the late 1990s. But during the pandemic in 2020 and 2021, the plight of the victims of cyber-crimes reached new heights. It was not online money theft only that was seen as the biggest problem of digitisation: there were violent crimes against women and children, hate crimes, political vandalism, intellectual property crimes etc., in cyberspace. Social media companies were alleged to fan online political hooliganism, the effect of which was felt in physical space also. Cyber-crime victims of different kinds of online criminal activities literally started standing without 'guardians' on several occasions, as the police and the criminal justice machinery were increasingly defeated by the cyber smart perpetrators, including the juveniles. Victims (especially individual victims) were met with rejection at the police station, as the police officers could not understand the ever-evolving patterns of cyber-crime victimisation. Most of the victims, especially women and victims of monetary fraud, were the recipients of victim blaming in police stations and the courts (in the event they were even able to reach out to the courts). Even if some prosecutors were successful in convincing the courts about the charges of the defendants, the courts were confused about the restoration of justice since the defendants never left the cyber space, even after they emerged from the correctional system and could emerge with new avatars.

Victimology expanded to include cyber-crime victimisations. As this book was being written, with the exception of the European Union Convention on Cybercrime, 2001 and its protocols, there were no conventions that addressed the issue of cyber-crime victimisation from the perspectives of general criminalities in cyberspace and the responsibilities of the State for law-making and extending mutual legal assistance with other countries. The General Data Protection Regulations, 2016 was yet another international document that emphasised the protection of data privacy. But victimhood in cyberspace has still remained a much-neglected subject in victimology. Today, there are millions of people who depend completely on the internet of things—and knowingly or unknowingly—they have shared their personal data with multiple industries and stakeholders. Nor are these companies risk free when it comes to safe archiving of the data. During the past few years we have seen ransom attacks on companies, industries and/or government institutions, which have had a devastating impact on ordinary individuals. Who is the primary victim here? Who can be blamed for negligence? Can the courts make all stakeholders happy? Queries are eternal. Here, discussions from a cyber victimological perspective may help stakeholders reach some decisions to help the victims.

This book provides a functional definition of Cyber Victimology. In the course of discussions on the patterns of cyber-crime victimisation, it also attempts to create a profile of the victims of cyber-crimes. Victimology cannot exclude discussions on the rights of the victims. Nor can Cyber Victimology exist without the discussions of the rights of the victims—including the Right to be Forgotten. Cyber Victimology necessarily considers the UN Declaration of the Basic Principles of Justice to Victims of Crimes and Abuse of Power to lay a pathway for policy-making for the victims of cyber-crimes. It also throws light on the issue of victim assistance for cyber-crime victims.

I hope that this book helps all to understand the plight and rights of victims of cyber-crimes from a transnational perspective. I also hope that this book may help frontline professionals in their understanding and assistance of cyber-crime victims.

Debarati Halder

LIST OF ABBREVIATIONS

CDA: Communication Decency Act, US
DMCA: Digital Millennium Copyright Act, US
EU: European Union
EUGDPR: European General Data Protection Regulations
UDHR: Universal Declaration of Human Rights
UK: United Kingdom
USA: United State of America
Vs: Versus

ACKNOWLEDGEMENTS

My mentors and friends from the International Society of Therapeutic Jurisprudence encouraged me to learn more about victimology in a very therapeutic way. I am honored to be a member of the board of trustees of this Society. Online discussions, seminars, and webinars were my virtual classrooms to learn from the veterans about therapeutic handling of the victims (irrespective of the pattern of crime victimisation) by frontline professionals and the courts. My sincere thanks to the entire trustee board of the International Society of Therapeutic Jurisprudence.

I was fortunate to be invited by companies like Facebook for their policy discussions on online safety of women and children. On numerous occasions, I would approach them on behalf of victims and request they consider bringing change to their policies to address issues of revenge porn, non-consensual image sharing, trolling, etc. I have learnt of the challenges these tech companies have to face. My sincere thanks to the policy measures team at Facebook, Instagram, and Twitter who explained their safety policies and even considered some of my suggestions for developing their own policies as well.

I humbly acknowledge the teachings of victimology veterans from the World Society of Victimology, South Asian Society of Victimology, and Indian Society of Victimology. My understandings about victimology grew with numerous sessions I attended at these academic societies.

My sincere thanks go to UNICEF for considering me worthy to be invited as a resource person for numerous meetings, training sessions, and discussions with government stakeholders on the online safety of adolescents. I learnt about the challenges that are needed to be addressed for the sake of the victims.

I humbly acknowledge the support and motivation of Mr. Ritesh Hada, Chairman, Karnavati University, Gandhinagar Gujarat, Dr. Deepak Shishoo, Hon'ble Provost of Karnavati University and my colleagues at the university.

My mother has been a silent support and a pillar of strength for me. Thank you Maa for letting me know how difficult it may be for senior citizens to become accustomed to the digital era. I can feel her generation's sense of helplessness when receiving phishing calls, sometimes leading to panic attacks. My twin sister deserves a special thanks here for her constant support.

My daughter was born in the digital era. When I started my work on Cyber Victimology, she was a minor. As a mother, I learnt how children enter into online gaming apps. She led me to understand the safety measures of gaming apps, how to upload reels on Insta and remain safe in cyberspace. As she steps into adulthood, I know I have something more to learn from her to understand what this young generation needs for a safe *new normal* life in cyberspace. I have no words to thank her: but I promise to be honest to her.

ABOUT THE AUTHOR

Prof (Dr.) **Debarati Halder**, LLB, ML, PhD (Law) (NLSIU, Bangalore)

Prof (Dr.) Debarati Halder is presently working with the Parul Institute of Law, Parul University, Gujarat, India. She has also worked with the Unitedworld School of Law, Karnavati University as a Full Professor. She is the founder and Honorary managing director of the Centre for Cyber Victim Counselling (CCVC) (www.cybervictims.org), an online not-for-profit organisation and a think tank meant for helping and counselling the victims of the internet and digital communication crime victims. She is the first law professor in India to introduce Therapeutic Jurisprudence as a subject as a credit course to LLB students.

Dr. Halder won two awards in 2019 for her work on cyber laws and gender rights, therapeutic jurisprudence, criminal laws, and creating awareness of cyber-crimes against women: these are the "Webwonderwomen Award" by the Ministry of Women & Children Affairs, Government of India & Twitter on 6th March, 2019 and the "TechNext India 2019 Best Faculty of the year" award by Computer Society of India, Mumbai Chapter on 28th September, 2019.

Dr. Debarati Halder has developed a theory called "Irrational Coping Theory for Online Victimisation," which is published as a book chapter entitled "Irrational Coping Theory and Positive Criminology: A Frame Work to Protect Victims of Cyber Crime" in the book *Positive Criminology*, (2015) edited by Natti Ronel and Dana Segav (Routledge, Taylor & Francis group, UK).

Dr. Debarati Halder, also works closely with intermediaries such as Facebook etc., government stakeholders like the National Commission for Women, State Commissions for Women and Commissions for Protection of Child Rights and Ministry of Information Technology, to help them shape new policy guidelines towards protection of women and children from online offences. She has also been invited by government stakeholders like the Bihar, Kerala, West Bengal, Tamil Nadu, Gujarat, Assam State Commissions for Protection of Child Rights, the Maharastra Commission for Protection of Women's Rights, etc., for imparting training to stakeholders committed for the protection of child rights. Dr. Halder has also assisted UNICEF India in creating child online safety-related materials, including the Child Online Protection in India (https://www.icmec.org/wp-content/uploads/2016/09/UNICEF-Child-Protection-Online-India-pub_doc115-1.pdf).

Dr. Debarati Halder is also the founding secretary of the South Asian Society of Criminology and Victimology (SASCV)(www.SASCV.org). She is also a member of the Board of Trustees of the International Society of Therapeutic Jurisprudence (https://www.intltj.com/).

Dr. Halder is an independent legal researcher. She has authored five books and edited one book including *Child Sexual Abuse and Protection Laws in India* (ISBN: 9789352806843) by Sage publications (2018), *Cyber Crime Against Women in India* (2016) by SAGE Publications, and *Cyber Crime and Victimisation of Women: Laws, Rights and Regulations* (2011), published by IGI Global, Hershey, P.A. Dr. Halder has also edited a book entitled *Therapeutic Jurisprudence and Overcoming Violence against Women* (2017) published by IGI Global, USA. Her book *Cyber Crime Against Women in India* (2016) by SAGE Publications has also been published in Hindi and Marathi by Sage Bhasha in 2019.

Dr. Halder is also the founder-Associate editor-Book review of two Scopus-UGC listed journals namely, the *International Journal of Cyber Criminology* (http://www.cybercrimejournal.com/) and the *International Journal of Criminal Justice Sciences* (www.http://www.sascv.org/ijcjs/index.html)

In addition to this, Dr. Debarati Halder has also published many scholarly articles on online victimisation of women, cyber law, child rights, therapeutic jurisprudence, human rights, prison rights of women, etc. in many national as well as international peer-reviewed journals and edited book chapters, including in the Routledge legal pedagogy series, the *British Journal of Criminology, International Annals of Criminology, National Law School Journal, Journal of Law and Religion* and many edited books including *Cyber Criminology, Social Networking as a Criminal Enterprise*, published by CRC press, Taylor & Francis Group.

Dr. Debarati Halder was also an invited speaker at the Stockholm Criminology Symposium, 2012. Dr. Debarati Halder is an expert resource person on cyber law, cybersecurity, cyber-crimes against women, online child protection and related laws, criminal laws, victimology, penology, etc. for many national and international policy-making bodies, including UNICEF, Facebook, National Commission for Women, West Bengal, Kerala and the Assam State Commission for Protection of Child Rights, the Maharastra State Commission for Women, etc. She has also been invited as an expert resource person by the courts and various institutes, including the Manipur High Court, the North Eastern Police Academy, Meghalaya, KIIT Law School, Bhubaneswar, Rajiv Gandhi Institute for Youth Development, Kancheepuram, Tamil Nadu, etc. She is also invited as resource person in many UGC assisted workshops and seminars.

Dr. Debarati Halder also served as Vice President for the Kids and Teens Division and Internet Safety advocate for Working to Halt Online Abuse (WHOA)(www.haltabuse.org) from 2008–2015.

1

INTRODUCTION

From Victimology to Cyber Victimology

1.1 Background

1.1.1 Victimology and Its Development

The study of victims and their participation in the causation of crime, the impact of their presence in the machinery for the administration of criminal justice has existed since ancient times. Ancient Indian scripts like the Manu Smriti and Arthashashtra touched upon the administration of victim justice.[1] The rights of victims were also recognised in Code of Hammurabi, which dates back to approximately 2000 BCE.[2] The ancient scripts emphasised the restoration of justice, compensation to the victim, and most importantly, the physical and mental well-being of the victims. These scripts however did not ignore the rights of the accused. But compared to the medieval and modern age, victims' rights were given more emphasis during ancient times. Much later, only in the twentieth century, French-Israeli defence lawyer Benjamin Mendelsohn began to look at the role of the victims in the causation of crimes. He was concerned about lowering the responsibility of the accused. In this way, he created a new wing of criminal law jurisprudence, i.e., 'victimology', the scientific study of victims, causes of victimisation, their relationship with criminals, etc. Following Mendelsohn's understanding of victimology, it was later explained as *"... the study of the etiology (or causes) of victimization, its consequences, how the criminal justice system accommodates and assists victims, and how other elements of society such as the media, deal with the crime victims."*[3] Mendelsohn divided the victims into six categories: (i) completely innocent victims, (ii) victims with minor guilt, (iii) victims as guilty as the offender. (iv) victims guiltier than the offender, (v) most guilty victim and (vi) imaginary victims.[4] Mendelsohn went on to explore how far this categorization of victims may lower the criminal responsibilities of the offender. Except the first category of victims, all others were considered as *contributors* to crime victimisation and this would go on to impact on their rights to compensation and restorative justice. At the same time, German criminologist Hans Von Hentig emphasised victim culpability and introduced even broader categorization of victims based on their gender, age, psychological aspects and their status in the geo-political-social region where they were residing when they had been exposed to the crime victimisation. As such, his 13 types of categorization of victims include the following: 1) the young; 2) the female; 3) the old; 4) the mentally defective and deranged; 5) immigrants; 6) minorities; 7) the dull normal; 8) the depressed; 9) the acquisitive; 10) the wanton; 11) the lonesome and the heartbroken; 12) the tormentors;

DOI: 10.4324/9781315155685-1

2 Introduction

and 13) the blocked, exempted, or fighting.[5] Hentig was the first to indicate that race and ethnicity played key roles in generating criminality in human beings.[6] Even though this categorization engendered huge debates and criticism, his theory of connecting race to criminality still applies in many jurisdictions. His detailed research on victim vulnerability showed that women and children and aged people must be given extra protection, and the liability should be shifted onto the State. Research on victimology aims to answer questions as to why certain classes of people become *victims* and why some other people do not become victims. Ezzat Fattah, a prominent representative of Positivist Victimology created seven categorizations for causation of victimisation in this regard. These are as follows: (i) opportunity for the criminals to access the victims, (ii) risk factors which may be found in gender, race, socio-cultural norms, (iii) presence of motivated offenders, exposure of the victims to the above-mentioned factors, (iv) associations of the victims which may place him or her in a situation to be victimised, (v) dangerous time and place which may make the victims more vulnerable, (vi) defensive behaviours of the victims and the criminals, (vii) structural and cultural proneness of being victimised.[7] Positivist victimology has been hugely criticised for shifting the blame onto the victims. The positivist theory of victimology relates to certain other victimological theories, which include Life Style Exposure Theory,[8] Routine Activity Theory,[9] and Victim Precipitation Theory.[10] Stephen Schafer, a criminologist and sociologist, pointed out in his 1967 work entitled "The Victim and His Criminal: Victimology",[11] that victims play a key role in contributing to their victimisation, particularly due to their own negligence, predisposition to victimisation, provocation to the offender/s, etc.

While all of the above-mentioned criminologists, victimologists, and sociologists were building their own theories on what leads a person to become a victim and how his or her relationship with the offender may contribute to the victimisation, the term 'victim' did not receive any universal definition until1985. The criminal law jurisprudence in most modern countries after Second World War was busy in accommodating the rights of the accused in the legal procedural systems. As the Universal Declaration of Human Rights (UDHR) in 1948 mandated, the responsibility of compensating the victims of war and political conflicts was being shifted to the wrongdoer governments, as seen in the Nuremberg Trials of 1945–1946.[12] But rather than considering the matter of compensating the victims, the tribunals were more concerned with framing forms of criminality. For victims of general crimes, the situation was no better. Primary victims were overshadowed by another class of victims, i.e., the State. Primary victims were reduced to mere witnesses who would be considered for their ability to provide the best witness testimony. Their stand as 'victims' in the guise of witnesses however would be affirmed on the basis of their testimony. This would mean that traumatised victims might not get the chance to establish their claims of victimhood as they might not cooperate properly with the prosecution due to their emotional and/or physical trauma. The more traumatised the victims, the better were the chances for the defendants to be acquitted from the charges because these 'best witnesses' would not be reliable in such cases then. But since the 1950s, certain States started considering creating policies and laws to support victim rights for rescue, rehabilitation, and compensation. John Dussich, in his phenomenal work, "The Evolution of International Victimology and Its Current Status in the World Today"[13] observed that from 1947 until 1985 a number of countries had taken steps to ensure victim justice through enacting laws for ensuring victim compensation, building shelter homes for female victims of domestic violence, and physical and sexual assaults, etc. This included countries like Israel, England, the United States, Canada, New Zealand, Australia, etc. The government in the United States started funding surveys on victims of unreported criminal activities.[14] This had tremendously helped in recognising new patterns of crime victimisations. Such surveys also empowered the 'hidden' victims to access justice. Israel and the United States also started national victims' rights weeks to generate more awareness among the victims and the criminal justice machinery.[15] Such state-funded measures helped the government and non-governmental stakeholders to reach out to the victims of racial and gender-based violence who were silenced due to socio-economic and political reasons.

But in practice, the treatment of victims and offenders by the police administration and the courts was largely being influenced by criminology, rather than victimology. The gravity of victimisation was being measured on the basis of physical violence and the amount of loss in property. Victims who had to undergo prolonged physical and emotional trauma and/or victims who had to undergo emotional and financial trauma due to death, disappearance, or permanent disablement of family members did not receive proper recognition. The government and the courts did not necessarily think about engaging frontline professionals, including restorative justice workers, psychologists, doctors, paramedics, and paralegal volunteers to make victims feel more comfortable in communicating with the courts about their pain and help them to recover from the trauma. This situation changed in 1985 when two landmark incidents happened in the field of victimology: (i) the introduction of the social coping theory of John Dussich,[16] which would show why victims of certain socio-economic strata may not survive as 'good victims,' due to their lack of capacity to cope with the situation, and (ii) the formation of the definition of the term 'victim' by the UN Declaration of Basic Principles of Justice for Victims of Crime and Abuse of Power, which took place in November, 1985.[17] The term 'victim' was explained and defined by this Declaration as follows:

> Victims means persons who, individually or collectively, have suffered harm, including physical or mental injury, emotional suffering, economic loss or substantial impairment of their fundamental rights, through acts or omissions that are in violation of criminal laws operative within Member States, including those laws proscribing criminal abuse of power............. A person may be considered a victim, under this Declaration, regardless of whether the perpetrator is identified, apprehended, prosecuted or convicted and regardless of the familial relationship between the perpetrator and the victim. The term "victim" also includes, where appropriate, the immediate family or dependants of the direct victim and persons who have suffered harm in intervening to assist victims in distress or to prevent victimization................... The provisions contained herein shall be applicable to all, without distinction of any kind, such as race, colour, sex, age, language, religion, nationality, political or other opinion, cultural beliefs or practices, property, birth or family status, ethnic or social origin, and disability.[18]

This definition expanded the scope to include victims of general crimes and victims of abuses of power. It also expanded the scope to include immediate family members who may have suffered, or would be suffering, due to the injury or loss suffered by the primary victims. The UN Declaration of Basic Principles of Justice for Victims of Crime and Abuse of Power (1985) also addressed victims' rights to access justice and receive fair and compassionate treatment from the criminal justice machinery and society as a whole. It also addressed victim-centred restitution of justice and victims' right to compensation.[19] It was the first international document to emphasise the victim impact statement and its role in the restitution of justice: Clause 6(b) of this declaration addresses this issue as follows:

> The responsiveness of judicial and administrative processes to the needs of victims should be facilitated by....... allowing the views and concerns of victims to be presented and considered at appropriate stages of the proceedings where their personal interests are affected,

4 Introduction

without prejudice to the accused and consistent with the relevant national criminal justice system;[20]

Post-1985, primarily because of the UN Declaration, several other stakeholders, including NGOs, academic-practitioner associations like the World Society of Victimology, etc. spoke out to suggest a stronger framework for victim justice. Such movements encouraged more crime reporting by crime victims irrespective of gender, race, nationality, and age. This had also impacted the consideration for right to assistance for crime victims. Academics and NGOs started emphasising the need for assistance to victims in accessing the criminal justice machinery for restitution of justice, and in availing themselves of compensation, accessing shelter homes, and securing police protection and no-contact orders from the courts in cases of acquittals or the release of the accused from custody on bail, etc. NGOs/civil society organizations were encouraged to create shelter homes on the basis of a public-private partnerships for victims. Victim justice programs became more organised with the introduction of the Basic Principles and Guidelines on the Right to a Remedy and Reparation for Victims of Gross Violations of International Human Rights Law and Serious Violations of International Humanitarian Law, 2005 (2005 guidelines).[21]

However, I argue that rights of the victims have not yet become stronger compared to that of the accused and the offenders. Even though government and civil society organizations have been vigorously campaigning for victims' rights, empowering the victims to access justice and holding legal literacy camps for adults and children to share awareness about rights and responsibilities, thousands of victims are still refused help at police offices. The problem of vanishing victims at the prosecution and trial level makes it impossible to achieve the goals of the 1985 Declaration and the 2005 guidelines. Victims—including those that are female, trans, children and belonging to minority groups—still lack the recognition and assistance that they deserve. Acquittals due to non-cooperation of the victims make the offender more powerful. The equilibrium between the rights of the victims and the accused/offender is never stable. Dussich's social coping theory beautifully portrays this. According to him, a person a may become a victim when his social coping mechanisms fail. Persons with few resources including socioeconomic resources, have a high likelihood of becoming victims of crime, social oppression, and abuse of power. As victims, they have poor chances of survival. If they survive at all, they may not recover.[22] The failure of the #MeToo movement could be the best example of Dussich's social coping theory in the contemporary world. A number of women across the globe spoke out against sexual harassment in the workplace. But not many of them could survive with their claim of victimhood. They had to withdraw their claims, either because they did not have proper evidence to support them during the court trials, or they were afraid of their very influential perpetrators. The victims feared for their lives, reputations, and survival in the job market because of their influential perpetrators, who could use their powerful networks to prevent the former from keeping their current job or accessing new job opportunities.[23] Victimology, therefore, needs more recognition in order to be understood and applied by the stakeholders for the sake of the victims.

1.2 Why Cyber Victimology?

With its tremendous growth since the millennium, crimes on the internet have increased over the years. Such crimes include machine-aided crimes like card fraud and cloning of cards; interpersonal and social media crimes, including cyberbullying, trolling, stalking, creation of revenge porn, online grooming, sexting and sextortion-related crimes, online gender violence, etc., and organised cyber-crimes, including cyberterrorism, child porn, copyright violation-related issues, etc. A number of criminologists, sociologists, psychologists, and legal researchers have identified various patterns of cyber-crime and possible causes for such criminal activities by applying criminological theories including Life Style Exposure theory, Routine Activity theory, Deviant Place theory, etc.[24] Several authors have also extensively researched the patterns of cyber-crimes against women and children from different jurisdictions,[25] content-related criminal activities on the internet,[26] cyberterrorism, cyber warfare, etc.[27] But few studies have been done on cyber-crime victims, their overall treatment by the criminal justice machinery, and the impact of cyber-crime victims on society as a whole. The majority of the literature on cyber-crimes, cybercriminology, and cyberlaws emphasise the possible reasons for the commission of crime, the modus operandi, and the possible consequences of the crime. Not much has been done to know why certain people may fall victims to certain specific types of cyber-crimes and how such a crime pattern may impact the psychological and physical well-being of the victim. There may be different layers of victimhood in certain cases of cyber-crimes. Consider the cases of phishing, where victims may unknowingly share their banking details with perpetrators: they may not feel victimised unless they receive information about unauthorised debits from their accounts through their phones or emails. In cases where the victims are digitally illiterate or senior citizens who may not be comfortable in using e-banking facilities, they may not know about their victimisation unless they are told about their loss by third parties or unless they are visiting the bank for other purposes and then learned about the loss. Women and children are considered the most vulnerable victims in cyberspace. There are countless examples of women being violated in cyberspace by different patterns of cyber-crimes. Women from socio-economically disadvantaged classes may be exploited in cyberspace by sex traffickers and porn content dealers in cyberspace. They may continue to be 'consumed' as porn content or, they may be trolled and their images shared multiple times without their consent for years.[28] These victims may remain ignorant of their victimisation. But when they come to know about their victimisation, it may instantly create multiple victims: family members of the primary victims may become secondary victims, either in suffering mental agony, or as a result of financial loss if their workplace reputations are affected due to the cyber victimisation of their women family members. Victims and their family members may even feel unprotected as their sensitive personal information may also become vulnerable to exploitation. In comparison to real life victimisation cases, compensation for online victimization may be less readily available. This may create anger and frustration in the victims. This may even create a motivation for the perpetrators to attack more victims with the same successful 'game plan' in the given criminal justice infrastructure. Children may be victimised by their peers and by the adults. The COVID lockdown period has seen the rise of online activities for children, including schooling. It was very disturbing to see schools across the globe failing to protect the online privacy of children. At the beginning of the worldwide lockdown, which started in March 2020, most schools had relied upon platforms like Zoom which itself was not prepared to handle the sudden increase of online meetings. There was chaos everywhere. Children were aware of the norms of online group discussions because they had been using Instagram and Snapchat for years before the lockdown begun. Adult teachers, however, could not manage the 'unruly 'classroom bullies who would take to the chat boxes to disrupt the ongoing classes. Some schools insisted on switching on the camera to make the children feel 'in the class' and monitor the behaviour of the children for discipline's sake. But this created problem of capturing images of girls and boys by their peers for using the same later for online harassment purposes. The home-quarantined children relied more on online games, including games displaying violence and porn. Before the parents and the governments could control the exposure of children to such games, which had allegedly impacted their behaviour, children had already

6 Introduction

become addicted to these contents. These instances could be shown as examples of victimless crimes in cyberspace. Stakeholders need to do more research on the impact of gaming apps, porn content, or social media on children. There are lacunae in victimological studies on these issues.

Cyber victimisation may even cause States to become victims. There can be cyber warfare,[29] cyberterrorism,[30] cyber espionage,[31] etc. The infamous 9/11 attack on the United States by the Taliban showed how the entire civil aviation computer infrastructure may be compromised by terrorist groups and how it may affect the national security of the country. In recent years, the world has witnessed how online radicalization for terrorist purposes has drastically affected adolescents, and in turn how the entire issue has forced global stakeholders to create laws and policies for restricting freedom of speech and expression and the right to information for all. The violation of intellectual property rights (IPR) is another segment of cyber victimisation which has often remained ignored by researchers of cyber-crimes. This issue has been considered as the subject matter of IPR laws. But in fact, this has a huge potential to be studied as part and parcel of cyber victimisation of individuals, corporate bodies, and States.

Most victimological studies have been limited by the common conclusion that victims did not receive proper care from the criminal justice machinery; due to jurisdictional issues, the crime remained undetected and the victim had to suffer emotional distress and financial loss. There are not many studies to show what sort of treatment was given to the victims by the courts during and after the trials. Simultaneously, few studies have been done to know whether or not the courts had passed any restraining orders against the perpetrator to restrain him from using the computer temporarily, whether or not the perpetrator had been fined or jailed for violating restriction orders to refrain from contacting the victim, whether or not the perpetrator could avail themselves of any other sort of defence, etc. For cases where States were victims of cyber-crimes, the victimhood of the States needs to be studied from a victimological perspectives as well. It may be seen that in such cases that although States remain the primary victims, citizens and aliens residing in the State may have to face numerous restrictions when it comes to access-ing public services, freedom of speech and expression, right to information, health services, etc. In such cases, the question that needs to be answered is, who should be treated as the victim? Often these 'victims' are re-victimised by the State which, in order to survive the attack and future attacks, may have to take extreme measures to curtain digital as well as real life rights of citizens. Based on cyberforensic tests, some States may be proclaimed as rogue States: they may be blacklisted and called terrorist states, and international stakeholders may decide to enact sanctions against them. In such cases, because of the 'accused status' of the State, the citizens in fact may be the 'victims' when it comes to the right to information, freedom of speech and information, and the right to access the internet. Internet companies may have operations in such countries and may try to run parallel governance here. But these may be considered illegal and the entire system of connectivity may be hampered giving the people at large a status of victimhood that may or may not be recognised by their courts of law.

Victimology, therefore, needs to be broadened to understand the plight of these victims. There are several forms of victimisation on the internet that have been termed as victimless crimes. These may include sexting,[32] certain phishing crimes, etc. where victims may become parts of the criminal network due to their ignorance. The criminal justice machinery may either ignore these victims, blame them, or treat them as offenders because the relevant evidence may not support their claims of victimhood. The situation must be handled after thoroughly know-ing the circumstances of when the victim had fallen into victimhood and how. Victim impact statements and careful reading and analysis of circumstantial evidences are key to understanding the situation in such cases. All these may necessarily be considered to expand the scope of victi-mology and adding cyber victimology as a new dimension of victimology.

1.2.1 Defining Cyber Victimology

The discussion in the above paragraph may suggest that cyber victimology is that discipline of victimology that studies victimological aspects of cyber-crimes. Broadly, *cyber victimology may be defined as the study of the causation of victimisation, patterns of victimisation and victimhood, the impact of victimisation, and the treatment of victims of cyber-crimes.*

The above-mentioned definition may therefore help to

Understand what is cyber victimisation

Know who may be vulnerable victims

Lean why such victims are vulnerable to cyber-crimes

Know the patterns of cyber victimisation

Learn about the impact of victimisation and predict what sorts of irrational and rational activities may be taken up by the victims of cyber-crimes

Identify who may be potential perpetrators for causing cyber victimisation

Understand the role of criminal justice machinery as a whole in dealing with cases of cyber victimisation.

Know about the impact of lack of laws, policy guidelines, criminal justice infrastructure on the society as a whole which may cause more cyber victimisation which may go undetected

Identify the need for private and public think tanks, policy makers, specialised branch of criminal justice system, including the prosecutors, judges, probation officers, prison officers, victim assistance stakeholders, etc., and their roles and functions.

1.2.2 Division of Chapters

This book aims to create a unique literature in the field of cyber victimology. In practice, it may be seen that often cases of cyber-crime victimisation are reported at an extremely late date to the criminal justice machinery, which makes it difficult for the police to ascertain what had happened to the victims. This may directly impact on restitution of justice because in most cases victims may have tried to resolve the issue in their own ways (the majority of which are illegal), which in turn may lead the victims to then be re-victimised.[33] This book therefore presents elaborate explanations on aspects of cyber victimology to enable readers to understand what is meant by cyber victimology, the patterns of cyber victimisation, and the profiling of the victims of cyber-crimes. It also discusses the rights of the victims in cyberspace, and issues and challenges of policing cyber-crimes from victimological angels. As well, this book includes discussions on victim assistance for the cyber-crime victims and penology for cyber-crimes with special reference to the application of Therapeutic Jurisprudence for victim healing.

The book opens with general discussions in the Introduction on the evolution of victimology as an area of study. Victimology is often said to be an offshoot of criminology. But it bears the heavy influence of criminal law jurisprudence as the proponents of victimology, who were defence lawyers themselves, primarily were interested in the issue of victim responsibility for the causation of crimes. Victimology was not born originally with the aim of making positive gains for victims. It was the other way around. Defence lawyers like Benjamin Mendelson investigated the issue of liabilities of the victims, which would reduce the criminal liability of the defendants. While researching this matter, lawyers such as Mendelsohn, Hans von Hentig, and Ezzat Fattah created categories of persons most likely to become victimised. Chapter 1 provides a concise look at such victim classifications made by different victimologists. These classifications will help the reader to understand why certain groups of people may attract victimisation in cyberspace

8 Introduction

as well. The chapter then discusses the Social Coping Theory of John Dussich, which relates to the powers of resilience and survival of the victims. This chapter then introduces the readers to the UN Declaration of Basic Principles of Justice for Victims of Crime and Abuse of Power, 1985, which for the first time introduced a uniform definition of 'victim'. It also throws light on the Basic Principles and Guidelines on the Right to a Remedy and Reparation for Victims of Gross Violations of International Human Rights Law and Serious Violations of International Humanitarian Law (2005), which expanded the scope of the 1985 Declaration, especially for the purpose of recognising rights of victims for remedy and reparation. This chapter then explains the reasons for introducing Cyber Victimology as a sub-school of Victimology. It has a very brief discussion on certain common forms of cyber-crimes and its victims. It then explains why cyber victimology is necessary to understand the plight and rights of victims. Finally, the chapter defines the term cyber victimology and explains the scope of the subject.

Chapter 2 discusses the patterns of cyber-crime victimisation, types of victims, the roles of victims and perpetrators in the causation of cyber victimisation and the profiles of the victims. With the development of time, patterns of cyber-crimes have expanded. It is no more confined to the concept of cyber espionage, unauthorised access to military commuters, or copyright violation of songs and movies. Data has become the costliest property any government, company, or human being may have. Cybercrime victimisation patterns now include data theft and illegal trading of data over the dark net. States are increasingly becoming victims of terrorism, including terrorism. Organised criminal gangs are targeting public transports and public properties. Before the States is able to take some preventive measures, the terrorist groups are able to access all information related to the civil aviation system and attack vulnerable places and people where predictive policing is less. They are able to run parallel governments and have a very strong web presence. They can manipulate the political maps available on the internet. They run web-based recruiting systems for drawing innocent individuals into their devastating hate propaganda campaigns. They use artificial intelligence to manipulate the emotional intelligence of people. Companies on the other hand are trying to build stronger infrastructure to secure the sensitive personal data of their customers and their own company secrets. However, they have to face the challenges of cybersecurity. Competition is no longer confined to the concept of market monopoly: companies are now competing with each other on the issue of business analysis and mapping of the consumers' mindsets for preference in products, brands and budgets. Many companies possess multiple layers of stakeholders for producing and marketing the internet of things. While such stuffs make the lives of people in the contemporary world more comfortable, this further generates huge data that needs more protection from the app creators, product manufacturers and dealers that are in direct connection with the consumers. All these stakeholders have been continuously targeted by perpetrators for ransom attacks on millions of data. They are victimised both by the perpetrators and the criminal justice system, as they are liable to pay compensation for their failure to protect the confidential information of their customers. Ordinary individuals experience different patterns of cyber-crime victimisation. It can be online hate propaganda, economic fraud, sexual offences, hacking, and the like. While the State and companies may be able to afford to protect their legal liabilities, ordinary individuals may not even be able to convince the police about the occurrence of the crime. Either they may not be digitally empowered, or they may not be sufficiently financially empowered to gather evidence to convince the criminal justice machineries about their plight. Chapter 2 discusses these aspects of cyber victimisation and provides a profile of the victims based on the available data on cyber-crime victimisation from the United States, the United Kingdom, India, and Australia.

Chapter 3 discusses rights in cyberspace. This is discussed under three headings: rights of the users of cyberspace, rights of the victims of cyber-crimes, and the right to be forgotten. The first category of rights is generally formulated on the basis of the Universal Declaration of Human Rights, the constitutional rights of citizens, and the rights created by the policy guidelines of the intermediaries for their users/subscribers/customers. These rights may be static if seen from the perspectives of the policy guidelines of different intermediaries and websites (most of which are hosted in the United States). But in certain aspects, these rights may vary according to the regional laws of different countries when it comes to freedom of speech and expression and accessing certain specific content in cyberspace. Both these forms of rights may influence the second category of rights, i.e., the rights of the victims of cyber-crimes. This can be considered as one of the core issues of cyber victimology. Victims' rights are multifaceted in this regard: they require removal of the content in question, confidentiality, restoration of lost reputation, as well as money and other compensation from the wrongdoers. Their rights also include the right to be protected from further harm. But how far is the same achievable when the victims may themselves have shared their own data? Chapter three discusses these issues. Rights in cyberspace must necessarily also include discussions on the right to be forgotten. This is a right for both the victims as well as the accused and the offenders. This chapter provides a detailed discussions of these key issues.

Chapter 4 of this book discusses the issue of policing cyber-crimes. There are two kinds of policing for any kind of crimes: one is moral policing. This is not generally supported by the legal machinery. The types of criminal activities that are covered by the moral police groups are generally related to social media activities of ordinary individuals, especially women and children. These may include uploading certain content on social media websites that may necessarily include still and audio-visual content. The second kind of policing is legal, and the police officers engaged by the State are responsible for controlling moral police groups as well. This chapter deals with the policing system concerning cyber-crimes supported by the law and justice machinery. Policing cyber-crimes is extremely challenging. It requires legal recognition of offences, training of the police officers and prosecutors to trace and handle the digital evidences, a proper infrastructure to preserve the evidence for prosecution purposes, and, above all, an awareness among the general public regarding cyber-crimes and proper reporting authorities. The problem of vanishing victims presents another big challenge for policing cyber-crimes. In the process of the administration of justice, States are increasingly including systems of electronic governance. In this, third parties may be involved for maintenance of the infrastructure, auditing of the security standards, etc. This third party may also have access to confidential court data. It becomes extremely challenging for the criminal justice machinery when such third parties leak such confidential data for illegal profit gain. Another significant challenge for policing crimes is jurisdictional issues. Even though the EU Convention on Cybercrime, 2001 had emphasised mutual legal assistance between State parties, in practice this may be extremely challenging. The absence of bilateral treaties between countries makes it impossible for police officers to gather evidence and arrest the offenders who may be taking shelter in different countries. This chapter presents detailed discussions of these issues.

Chapter 5 deals with victim assistance for cyber-crime victims. The 1985 UN Declaration and the 2005 Principles and Guidelines emphasised victim assistance for victims of crimes and abuse of power. Cybercrime victims need assistance as well. Such assistance includes assistance in accessing justice, recovery of the data from the hackers, content removal from the web, protection from the perpetrator from future harm, compensation from the perpetrator—including the tech companies that may have been negligent in responding to the reports made by the victims, and so on. Assistance also includes rescue and rehabilitation: there are victims who may be victimised in cyberspace as well as in physical space. These may include victims of online trafficking. Even if they may be rescued from the traffickers' dens or porn dens, their data and

10 Introduction

images may remain accessible for further exploitation in the deep dark web. Victim assistance in cyber-crime victimisation cases cannot confined to the police or the courts. It should be a collective effort of stakeholders, including the tech companies, NGOs, and the criminal justice system. Chapter 5 discusses in detail victim assistance from all these perspectives.

Chapter 6 speaks about penology in cyber-crime victimisation cases. The EU Convention on Cybercrime, 2001 has recognised certain types of cyber-crimes. As discussed above, these offences have expanded in nature. There are multiple types of hate crimes, economic crimes, data theft, sexual offences, attacks on protected systems of the government, etc. Offenders are not always adults. Children are also committing offences in cyberspace. There are organised gangs who are expanding into new areas in all jurisdictions. Numerous cyber-crime offences have a deep impacted on the physical safety of the victims. Adolescents and young adults have committed suicide because they had been 'instructed' to kill themselves as parts of online games. Online platforms hosting the 'games' did not want to take liability for deaths in real life. But they cannot escape their liability for not being able to monitor such activities on their own platforms. What sort of punishments may be awarded to them? Can the victims benefit from such punishments? In practical terms, there are no uniform answers for such questions because the courts are still adjusting to them with ever-evolving patterns of criminalities taking place in cyberspace. Existing domestic laws have a set of punishments for some common patterns of crime victimisation. These punishments include jail terms and fines. Certain countries have included no-contact orders or prohibitory orders in their penal codes relating to cyber-crime cases. But these forms of punishments may vary according to the age of the offenders and impact of the offences on the victims, as well as the society at large. Courts need to be innovative while awarding punishment for cyber-crime offences. They should include remedial measures for the victims as well. Above all, the courts should adhere to the principles of therapeutic jurisprudence for healing of the victims. Penology for cyber-crimes should be necessarily victim-oriented. Reformation of the offenders is considered to be a permanent component of penology. But penology for cyber-crime victimisation must also concern virtual avatars of the defendants and the victims. Anonymity is a challenge in the control of cyber-crime. Courts must consider roping in the tech companies to implement the prohibitory orders. Further, the courts must also set guidelines for community sentences for adolescents and young adults in cyber-crime cases. Penology for cyber-crimes must also include rehabilitation programs for offenders, which should include de-addiction from violent content, porn content, etc. All these issues are discussed in Chapter 6.

Chapter 7 provides the conclusion to the book. This chapter discusses what cyber victimology may offer to students, as well as to practitioners and frontline professionals dealing with victims of cyber-crime. This chapter also explains how the principles of the UN Declaration of Basic Principles of Justice for Victims of Crime and Abuse of Power may be expanded to assist victims of cyber-crimes.

Notes

1 See Jaishankar, K., & Halder, D. (2019) Criminal justice tenets in Manusmriti: A critical appraisal of the ancient Indian Hindu code. In K. Jaishankar (Ed.), *Routledge handbook of South Asian criminology*. pp. 97–110. ISBN: 9780429320118.

2 See Schafer, S. (1970). Victim compensation and responsibility. *Southern California Law Review, 43*, 55.

3 See Deigle, L.E. (2017). *Victimology: The essentials*. Sage Publications.inc. ISBN: 9781506388519. Also see https://uk.sagepub.com/sites/default/files/upm-binaries/83271_Chapter_1.pdf. Accessed on 09.09.2020.

4 Arifi, B. (2016). Categorization of crime victims: comparing theory and legislation. *Temida, 19*(3–4), 493–515. Available at http://www.doiserbia.nb.rs/Article.aspx?id=1450-66371604493A#.X7DNA 8gzaM8. Accessed on 09.09.2020.

5 Dussich, J. (2015). The evolution of international victimology and its current status in the world today. *Revista de Victmologia/Journal of Victimology*, 1(1). Available at: https://www.researchgate.net/publication/281032052_The_Evolution_of_International_Victimology_and_its_Current_Status_in_the_World_Today_Revista_de_Victmologia_Journal_of_Victimology_Volume_1_issue_1_2015. Accessed on 22.07.2021].

6 Von Hentig, H. (1940).Criminality of the negro. *Journal of Criminal Law and Criminology, 30*(5), 662–680.Available at https://scholarlycommons.law.northwestern.edu/cgi/viewcontent.cgi?article=2905 &context=jclc.Accessed on 09.09.2020.

7 Miers, D. (1989). Positivist victimology: A critique. *International Review of Victimology*, 1(1), 3–22. Available at https://www.researchgate.net/profile/David_Miers/publication/284706920_Positivist_Victimology_A_Critique/links/5bee97e4a6fdcc3a8dda19a3/Positivist-Victimology-A-Critique.pdf. Accessed on 09. 09.2020.

8 Madero-Hernandez, A. (2019). Lifestyle exposure theory of victimization. In Frances P. Bernat, Kelly Frailing, Loraine Gelsthorpe, Sesha Kethineni, & Lisa Pasko (Eds.), *The encyclopedia of women and crime*. pp. 1–3. Available at https://onlinelibrary.wiley.com/doi/abs/10.1002/9781118929803.ewac0334. Accessed on 09.09.2020.

9 Felson, M. (2008). Routine activity approach. In Richard Wortley & Lorraine Mazerolle (Eds.), *Environmental criminology and crime analysis*. Pp. 92–99. Willan.

10 Curtis, L.A. (1974). Victim precipitation and violent crime. *Social Problems, 21*(4), 594–605. Also see Cortina, L.M. (2017). From victim precipitation to perpetrator predation: Toward a new paradigm for understanding workplace aggression. In N.A. Bowling & M.S. Hershcovis (Eds.), *Current perspectives in social and behavioral sciences. Research and theory on workplace aggression* (pp. 121–135). Cambridge University Press. https://doi.org/10.1017/9781316160930.006. URL: https://psycnet.apa.org/record/2017-50124-005. Accessed on 09.09.2020.

11 See for more information, https://play.google.com/books/reader?id=4uPTjld8C50C&hl=en&pg=GBS. PP3. Accessed on 09.09.2020.

12 After the Second World War, there were a series of military trials held at Nuremberg by the allied forces to consider the responsibility of the Nazi forces in the severe violation of the laws of war and human rights. This series of trials is considered to represent a landmark in the history of international law and the laws of war. In addition to holding the Nazis responsible for international war crimes, including the Holocaust, these trials were among the first cases to consider the rights of the victims. For more information, see Taylor, T. (1955). The Nuremberg Trials. *Columbia Law Review*, 55(4), 488–525.

13 Dussich, J.P. (2015). The evolution of international victimology and its current status in the world today. *Revista de victimología*, (1), 37–81. Available at https://dialnet.unirioja.es/descarga/articulo/5774195.pdf. Accessed on 10.09.2020.

14 Ibid.

15 Ibid.

16 Dussich, J. P. (1985). *New perspectives in control theory: social coping of youth under supervision*. Köln: Heymanns.

17 See Declaration of Basic Principles of Justice for Victims of Crime and Abuse of Power. Accessible from https://www.un.org/en/genocideprevention/documents/atrocity-crimes/Doc.29_declaration%20 victims%20crime%20and%20abuse%20of%20power.pdf Accessed on 09.09.2020.

18 Ibid.

19 Ibid.

20 See in ibid.

21 Detailed discussions of this guideline are given in Chapter 5 of this book.

22 Revista de VICTIMOLOGIA. *Journal of Victimology*, 37–81. ISSN 2385-779Xwww.revistadevictimologia. com | www.journalofvictimology.com. https://doi.org/10.12827-RVJV-1-02.

23 For example, see Tim Bower. (2019). *The #MeToo Backlash*. Published in https://hbr.org/2019/09/the-metoo-backlash. Accessed on 21.10.2020.

24 For example, see Leukfeldt, E.R., & Yar, M. (2016). Applying routine activity theory to cybercrime: A theoretical and empirical analysis. *Deviant Behavior, 37*(3), 263–280. Available at https://www.tandfonline.com/doi/pdf/10.1080/01639625.2015.1012409. Accessed on 21.10.2020; Yar, M. (2005). The Novelty of 'Cybercrime' An Assessment in Light of Routine Activity Theory. *European Journal of Criminology, 2*(4), 407–427. Available at https://d1wqtxts1xzle7.cloudfront.net/43681131/The_Novelty_of_CybercrimeAn_Assessment_i20160313-2737-st7szn.pdf?1457872238=&response-content-disposition=inline%3B+filename%3DThe_Novelty_of_Cybercrime_An_Assessment.pdf& Expires=1605631286&Signature=LnEJPg59uIj4CPQiskUYq2JnASVrRlTaBNyTSNAATlO2XMzsu ZTtIysI7cqcN3hPAc74z2N~JN8aOUyhBiZWHND3UCBeGTWwgvkDq8dwu4llg3~7pmrcsYzHZ 4m4aSwkYH~dyjPmXHylHCtRf~7Wgvq80cLao5RgCEKdJ0BEZ9V07j9qA7uNoU8tT5p~IJd9P 9s0hhDKCMvuI3CrQ5vlVb4Ixlc9pu2zgsKONfyC6cDSpE~W1KquCnnJ4vd~r2M-VFcmR3g

DW1mcvJsIFf8X9MqYlLPZN8k~p7u7r82cJa8WPo2DFPkv3taN~0au4r-4AOlqNBus4etmx3Sbp
yAVAw__&Key-Pair-Id=APKAJLOHF5GGSLRBV4ZA. Accessed on 21.10.2020; Reyns, B.W., &
Henson, B. (2016). The thief with a thousand faces and the victim with none: Identifying determinants
for online identity theft victimisation with routine activity theory. *International Journal of Offender Therapy and Comparative Criminology, 60*(10), 1119–1139. Available at https://d1wqtxts1xzle7.cloudfront.
net/44358325/Reyns__Henson__2015_GSS_IDENTITY_THEFT.pdf?1459703301=&response-
content-disposition=inline%3B+filename%3DThe_Thief_With_a_Thousand_Faces_and_the.
pdf&Expires=1605631371&Signature=EtKGixiaezaMWKbypfNsD-NdcheDrw6arpM1WZC4w
wO5MniOlFqxO16dUMcWzTsEK71oA~Vi6ckWoAtJZLtnnUYt-kQgXEdfjOu0U5Re250Ljl
RGc-QKLyKuh~fSa3EPZeFOdgD59gJxT3ZQP-OlSMYzEabXrb0QhEmeTPDIGAORQVDkxP
Bl9gtuCoYvoR63RCSD8jOD003qRTZvPBnp4Myet3Ld7YTptI9~ae3oewUap9SWscrqyRiC9dQn
FGlTrRxOG0bfYr6mzVJGU3Jr3Mbb4RaBPvzMCCAgRkdlKlzsmYjJR7ESd1cIOfsfSB8z4aHydVz
t9nnme9Wsh3jCQ__&Key-Pair-Id=APKAJLOHF5GGSLRBV4ZA. Accessed on 21.10.2020.

25 Halder D., & Jaishankar, K (2016.) *Cyber crimes against women in India.*
New Delhi: SAGE Publications. ISBN: 9789385985775; Halder D., & Jaishankar, K. (2012). *Cyber crime and
the victimization of women: Laws, rights, and regulations.* Hershey, PA, USA: IGI Global.
ISBN: 978-1-60960-830-9; Halder D., & Jaishankar K. (2016) Celebrities and cyber crimes: An analysis of
the victimization of female film stars on the internet. *Temida—The Journal on Victimization, Human Rights
and Gender, 19*(3–4), 355–372.
ISSN: 14506637; Halder D., & Jaishankar, K. (2014). Online victimization of Andaman Jarawa tribal
women: An analysis of the 'human safari' YouTube videos (2012) and its effects. *British Journal of Criminology, 54*(4), 673–688. ISSN: 00070955; Halder, D., & Jaishankar. (2013). Revenge porn by teens in the
United States and India: A socio-legal analysis. *International Annals of Criminology, 51*(1–2), 85–111. ISSN:
00034452; Halder, D., & Jaishankar, K. (2011). Cyber gender harassment and secondary victimization: A
comparative analysis of US, UK and India. *Victims and Offenders, 6*(4), 386–398. ISSN: 15564886; Halder,
D., & Jaishankar K. (2009, September). Cyber socializing and victimization of women. *Temida—The Journal
on Victimization, Human Rights and Gender, 12*(3), 5–26. ISSN: 14506637; Citron, D.K. (2009). Cyber civil
rights. *Boston University Law Review, 89*, 61; Citron, D.K. (2009). Law's expressive value in combating cyber
gender harassment. *Michigan Law Review, 108*, 373; Citron, D.K. (2019). Cyber mobs, disinformation, and
death videos: The internet as it is (and as it should be). *Michigan Law Review, 118*, 1073; Citron, D.K., &
Wittes, B. (2018). The problem isn't just backpage: Revising section 230 immunity. Citron, D.K., & Franks,
M.A. (2019). Evaluating New York's "revenge porn" law: A missed opportunity to protect sexual privacy;
Franks, M.A., & Waldman, A.E. (2018). Sex, lies, and videotape: Deep fakes and free speech delusions.
Maryland Law Review, 78, 892.

26 Holt, T.J., Freilich, J.D., & Chermak, S.M. (2017). Exploring the subculture of ideologically motivated
cyber-attackers. *Journal of Contemporary Criminal Justice, 33*(3), 212–233.; Holt, T.J., Strumsky, D., Smirnova,
O., & Kilger, M. (2012). Examining the social networks of malware writers and hackers. *International Journal
of Cyber Criminology, 6*(1).

27 Kenney, M. (2015). Cyber-terrorism in a post-Stuxnet world. *Orbis, 59*(1), 111–128; Wall, D.S. (2015). The
internet as a conduit for criminal activity. In A. Pattavina (Ed.), *Information technology and the criminal justice
system* (pp. 77–98).

28 See for example in Halder D., & Jaishankar, K. (2014). Online victimization of Andaman Jarawa tribal
women: An analysis of the 'human safari' YouTube videos (2012) and its effects. *British Journal of Criminology, 54*(4), 673–688. (Impact factor 1.556). ISSN: 00070955.

29 Dipert, R.R. (2010). The ethics of cyberwarfare. *Journal of Military Ethics, 9*(4), 384–410.

30 Stohl, M. (2006). Cyber terrorism: a clear and present danger, the sum of all fears, breaking point or
patriot games? *Crime, Law and Social Change, 46*(4–5), 223–238. Available at https://www.researchgate.
net/profile/Michael_Stohl/publication/227324608_Cyber_Terrorism_A_Clear_and_Present_Danger_
the_Sum_of_All_Fears_Breaking_Point_or_Patriot_Games/links/0fcfd50c01eade053e000000/Cyber-
Terrorism-A-Clear-and-Present-Danger-the-Sum-of-All-Fears-Breaking-Point-or-Patriot-Games.pdf.
Accessed on 12.09.2020.

31 Deibert, R.J., Rohozinski, R., Manchanda, A., Villeneuve, N., & Walton, G.M. F. (2009). Tracking Ghost-
Net: Investigating a cyber espionage network. Available at https://ora.ox.ac.uk/objects/uuid:6d1260fd-
b8ee-4a11-8a5f-e7708d543651/download_file?safe_filename=Gh0stNet.pdf&file_format=application%
2Fpdf&type_of_work=Report. Accessed on 12.09.2020.

32 Halder, D., & Jaishankar, K. (2013). Revenge porn by teens in the United States and India: A socio-legal
analysis. *International Annals of Criminology, 51*(1–2), 85–111.

33 Halder, D., & Jaishankar, K. (2015). Irrational coping theory and positive criminology: A frame work to
protect victims of cyber crime. In N. Ronel and D. Segev (Eds.), *Positive criminology* (pp. 276 –291). Abingdon, Oxon: Routledge. ISBN: 978-0-415-74856-8.

2

PATTERNS OF CYBER VICTIMISATION AND THE ROLE OF VICTIMS AND PERPETRATORS

2.1 General Patterns of Cyber-Crime Victimisation

2.1.1 Introduction

This is the age of internet. E-governance, e-commerce, and information communication technology are shaping personal relationships more than ever. The 2020 COVID-19 pandemic made the entire world overdependent on information communication technology. But internet-based communication including e-governance, e-commerce, and the like has long been accepted as the norm by the global community. A brief history of the internet would suggest that computer-based works and communications, including digitizing military intelligence related documents in the United States, involving universities in the development of a stronger digital infrastructure for securing national security-related information in the 1960s, led to *soft* tensions between superpowers like the United States and the then Soviet Union. Slowly, the superpowers started expanding their nuclear powers and this involved the quick development of the digitisation of the military and government intelligentsia in several other countries. By the mid-1980s, when Apple stepped into the market as the would-be computer electronics and software company giant, several economically and politically influential states became targets of non-state actors who would target the government cyberinfrastructure because of the vulnerability of the said infrastructure. University students started hacking protected devices, music piracy became rampant, and governments in many countries started outsourcing responsibilities of maintenances of cybersecurity infrastructures, making the situation even more complex.[1] By late 1990s, when internet companies like Yahoo started appearing, government as well as governmental stakeholders adopted internet technology-based communications to exchange confidential information with the help of email service providers, some of which were supported by such internet companies. This system enormously facilitated overseas government, commercial, and interpersonal communications. During this time, Lawrence Lessig advocated for a universally acceptable structure for cyberlaw that would emphasise cross-border issues.[2] The early millennium years saw the rise of several forms of cyberattacks, including malware attacks, which would further facilitate crimes like Trojan attacks, ransomware attacks, etc.[3] Several sophisticated criminal gangs also turned to the development of organised cyber-crimes, which included using a denial of service Attack (DoS), distributed denial of service attacks (DDoS), economic crimes, cyberespionage, cyberterrorism, etc. This was just the beginning of

DOI: 10.4324/9781315155685-2

14 Patterns of cyber victimisation

an era that would see the gradual increase of different types of cyber-crimes targeting governments, companies, and ordinary individuals. For the first time, in 2001, the EU Convention on Cybercrime (also known as the Budapest Convention) recognised certain types of cyber offences. This convention categorised cyber-crimes into four categories as follows:

i   Offences against confidentiality, integrity and availability of the computer data and system which included illegal access, interference with data, devices and the networking system as a whole, illegal interception, misuse of devices, which includes illegal sale, theft, etc., of the device, password etc.[4]
ii Computer related offences, which includes computer related forgery, which may result in production of inauthentic data for illegal profit gain and duping others and computer fraud which may cause loss including wide scale financial loss to others.[5]
iii Content related offences, which includes child pornography related offences.[6]
iv Offences related offences including copyright infringement and related rights.[7]

But later, the international stakeholders broadened the scope of this Convention and recognised several other offences: these included the offence of racist and hate crime propaganda through the Internet which was addressed in the Additional Protocol to the Convention on Cybercrime, concerning the criminalisation of acts of a racist and xenophobic nature committed through computer systems, 2003,[8] the terrorist offence of using cyberspace for recruiting and training of terrorists through the Council of Europe Convention on Prevention of Terrorism, 2005,[9] the sexual exploitation and abuse of children via the Internet through the Council of Europe Convention on the Protection of Children against Sexual Exploitation and Sexual Abuse (Lanzarote Convention, 2007),[10] etc. Data privacy-related issues and criminal activities were later addressed by the EU General Data Protection Regulation, 2016.[11]

This chapter will discuss different patterns of cyber-crime victimisation. It will next create a profile of the victims of cyber-crimes. This profiling will be helpful in understanding why certain patterns of cyber-crimes are targeted to certain specific types of victims.

2.1.2 General patterns of cyber-crime victimisation

A number of research efforts suggest that there are primarily three kinds of victims of cyber-crimes; namely the State, companies, and ordinary individuals (Kshetri, 2005;[12] Wall, 2007;[13] Halder & Jaishankar, 2016).[14] There can be certain unique patterns of victimisation targeting these three kinds of victims. These are as below:

Cyberterrorism

Sri Lanka was considered to be one of the first States to be attacked by cybercriminals at the end of the 1990s. Due to the ethnic war in Sri Lanka, the Liberation Tigers of Tamil Eelam (LTTE) became the prime target of the government. The physical war could have been controlled by the Sri Lankan government. But several members of the LTTE, and its Sri Lankan Tamil supporters who had sought refuge in other jurisdictions, continued to support the battle by engaging in developing alternative cyberattack strategy. By 1998, the 'Black Tigers', a terror organisation allegedly affiliated with LTTE, sent 800 emails to various embassy websites of Sri Lanka, which impacted heavily on the information technology-based government communication. Seen from the perspective of 2020, this might not seem to be a problem any government or private email service provider and recipient/s could not handle. But email communication systems were not as sophisticated as they are now. This email bombing of the government was a new kind of terror activity, which led to several non-state actors taking greater measures, by way of cyberterrorism, to attack government data and cyberinfrastructure. Denning (2000) very articulately defined this phenomenon in the following words:

> Cyberterrorism is the convergence of terrorism and cyberspace. It is generally understood to mean unlawful attacks and threats of attack against computers, networks, and the information stored therein when done to intimidate or coerce a government or its people in furtherance of political or social objectives. Further, to qualify as cyberterrorism, an attack should result in violence against persons or property, or at least cause enough harm to generate fear. Attacks that lead to death or bodily injury, explosions, plane crashes, water contamination, or severe economic loss would be examples. Serious attacks against critical infrastructures could be acts of cyberterrorism, depending on their impact. Attacks that disrupt nonessential services or that are mainly a costly nuisance would not.[15]

Soon this became one of the burning security issues for international organisations as well as state parties. It has led to numerous treaties and conventions for joint actions against cyberterrorism.[16] By the first half of the millennium, several other countries had suffered attacks on their cyberinfrastructure. For example, consider the case of Al Qaeda, who conducted the 9/11 attack on the World Trade Center and Pentagon office in the United States in 2001. Several researchers have opined that this serves as the biggest example involving computer technology to systematically plan terror attacks.[17] Soon after this, Estonia encountered a distributed denial-of-service attacks (DD-o-S) by perpetrators in 2007. The government websites were badly affected and this caused serious damage to the cyberinfrastructure of the Estonian government. Investigations revealed that this was mainly due to the Estonian government's action of moving a Russian war memorial statue to a military cemetery. The offline fury between ethnic groups took its toll on the cyberinfrastructure, which was controlled only when the United States and NATO actively helped Estonia to control the damage.[18] But this cannot be considered as a very good example of cyberterrorism: there were more to come. From 2007–2008 onwards cyberterrorism grew tremendously under the leadership of ISIS.[19] The Islamist fundamentalists have a robust internet presence now. They have their own administrative structure. They have occupied parts of countries like Syria and Iraq and their websites claimed that they have been running a successful Caliphet.[20] The internet is flooded with the revamped political maps of the countries that have been affected by ISIS operations. They have their own social media handles, despite being called out by various States and international organisations as terrorist organisations, and they have well-trained recruiters, who through their own websites and other social media handles, regularly call for young people to join the organisation.[21] Encouraged by the success of ISIS, several other separatist groups have also created their own web spaces and often take responsibility for organised terror attacks, including cyberterrorism in a number of jurisdictions.[22] In the case of cyberterrorism the ultimate aim of the terrorists is widespread destruction and damage to human lives, as well as to properties owned by government and civilians. The terror organisations may avail themselves of different modus operandi to access confidential government data, disrupt digital and icommunication services, access the government operation of transport and communication systems—including aviation services—and may cause a wide range of violence. Apart from using computers, data, and computer network services for causing physical violence, they may also attack the government websites, then proceed to deface them and engage in ransomware attacks for monetary gain as well as gain access to confidential data, etc,. As discussed above, several prominent terror organisations have robust social media operators, who may play

16 Patterns of cyber victimisation

key roles in floating information about the organisation in different social media platforms and webpages, recruiting people for achieving the goals of the terror outfits, and developing means of profit gain by using the social media companies. People responsible for these activities often work so vigorously and on so many different levels, that even if the social media company or the concerned web domain company was alerted about the usage of their platforms for terrorist purposes, the former might immediately create another page or share more information in the event the latter pulled down the contents on the grounds of terrorism. Cyberterrorists, therefore, may target both the governments and companies, especially internet companies. The latter may face two-way victimisation: if the company is unable to take down the terrorism-related content, nation states—which may be victimised due to the operation of the terror outfits on the basis of the services provided by web companies in their jurisdiction—may make the companies criminally liable. On the other hand, due to an 'anonymous veil', the members of the terror organisations may repeatedly return to create more content on the said web platforms, thereby making the web companies perpetually liable for hosting illegal content.

Cyberwarfare and attack on government data

While in the above cases the State is targeted by non-state actors, terror groups, and criminal gangs who engage in crime for illegal gains, States may also be targeted by other States. The development of a specific computer worm named Stuxnet during the early years of the millennium by a US-Israeli partnership (backed by their respective governments) to deliberately delay the Iranian nuclear program introduced very sophisticated cyberwarfare between States that often received a sympathetic response because of its purpose—namely to delay or destroy a particular State's efforts to develop nuclear programs for military warfare.[23] These activities necessarily included cyber espionage, infecting other computers, and accessing without authorization computers, networks, data, etc. But this should not be confused with cyberterrorism, which is performed by separatist non-state actors. Again, there can be individual groups or individual hackers who may carry out web hijacking and web defacement of government websites. There are hundreds of examples of this, including web defacement cases involving India-Pakistan, Indo-China, China-US, Indo-Sri Lanka, China-Taiwan Israel-Palestine, etc.[24] The majority of such attacks may not be directly supported by the 'enemy country.' But in certain instances the political embarrassment due to web defacement and web hijacking may serve as leverage in diplomatic tussles between the *not-so-friendly* countries. These hackers may act as hidden agents for cyber espionage as well. The data that may be collected by way of hacking of government websites, which may necessarily include data of national interest, the financial data of ordinary individual tax payers, health data, etc., may be sold in the dark web world for huge monetary gain. One of the greatest examples of this is the WannaCry ransomware attack on the United Kingdom's National Health Services data in 2017, which later affected many other government and private hospital data worldwide.[25]

The above discussion may provide a representative understanding of governments as victims of cyber-crimes. However, considering that the State is an abstract concept without its people, it must be noted that attacks on cyberinfrastructures of the government ultimately lead to attacks on individuals residing in that State. The layers of victimisation in such cases may be understood in the following flow chart (Figure 2.1):

Unauthorised access to computers, data, etc.

Unauthorised access to computers, data network, etc., is considered to be one of the earliest detected computer crimes, whereby perpetrators may access or attempt to access computers and

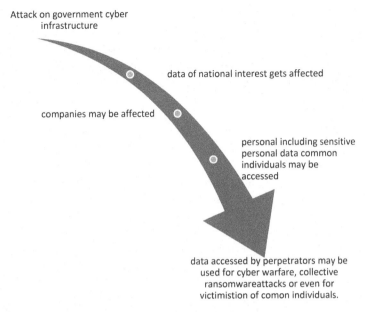

FIGURE 2.1 Layers of victimisation

the confidential data stored in the concerned devices. This type of criminal activity is closely connected with cyberterrorism and cyber warfare, as discussed above. In general, unauthorised access to computers, data, etc., has been considered a privacy-breaching related crime.[26] The main motive is to access data for illegal gain. The modus operandi may necessarily include attacking devices that may store confidential data related to national security, financial data, etc. Unauthorised access to data, devices, etc., may also include unauthorised modification of data. The entire operation of unauthorised access to devices, data, and modification of the content is popularly known as hacking.[27] Hackers and crackers may operate to access confidential data and attack the entire system for denial of services (DoS) or dedicated denial of services (DDoS) so that no information may be communicated through the affected computer and the affected computer may become dysfunctional.[28] Computers and computer systems used for government purposes may be the soft targets of the hackers as they may gain unethical profits by way of misusing confidential data. There are certain computers and computer systems that are designated as 'protected computers'. These computers may have significant confidential data because they are connected with important financial institutions, mostly involved with interstate commerce, or with government in such a way that the unauthorised access to such devices, or data, or the computer network system may directly affect interstate or foreign commerce, or core government activities, including the voting system and national security.[29] Apart from these, the hackers and crackers may also proceed to attack or help to attack maritime cybersecurity, as well as the cyberinfrastructure that addresses governance of space and aeronautics.[30] The primary regulation for addressing unauthorised access to computer, data, etc., in the United States is 18 U.S. Code § 1030, which deals with fraud and related activities in connection with computers. This provision prohibits intentional access and breach of confidentiality of computers and data, including protected computers that are confidential for government purposes, intentional damage to the said computer/s, data, etc., and disruption to communication traffic which may in consequence affect the security and confidentiality of the State, as well as interstate and international commerce. A brief reading of the provision would also show that emphasis is given to prior knowledge of the wrongdoer about the importance of the computer, data, etc., that he or she wishes to unauthorisedly access.[31] A clear reading of this legal provision would also show that the scope of the provision extends to threats to commit the offence, ransom attacks, conspiracy to commit the offence/s and attempts to commit the offence/s. The United Kingdom also has penalised such activities of unauthorised access to computers, including protected computers, data, intentional disruption of communication traffic, and damaging or destroying the computers and data which are used for government purposes through the *Computer Misuse Act*, 1990 (CMA).[32] The English law also places heavy significance on the types of consequences that may result due to the unauthorised access to the computer and data under S.3ZA: it includes within its scope the criminal activities and injuries which may cause loss of life, serious injury, financial loss to the government and public at large, hamper public welfare-related activities, etc.[33] Similar provisions for penalising unauthorised access to computer, data, etc., can be found in several other countries, including Singapore,[34] Australia,[35] Canada,[36] India,[37] etc. Unauthorised access to data and DoS and DDoS attacks may also lead to cyber espionage and cyberterrorism.

Interestingly, two specific connotations may be made here with the State as a major repository of data: (a) because the government may be considered as a repository of sensitive personal data of the people living in the State, any sort of unauthorised access may give the data owner/s a broader right to sue the government for negligence for failure to maintain security for such data. However, in most of the cases, sensitive personal data may be taken care of by third parties who may be commissioned by the government. Hence, the government may shift the liability of negligence for failure to ensure proper cybersecurity to the data to such third-party body corporates. (b) the State may be victimised as an independent unit, especially when interstate commerce activities and confidential data about the security of the nation—including the military intelligentsia, etc.—are breached. Even though this may also affect the lives of people living within the State, the latter could definitely be provided victim status in this regard.

Attack by way of unauthorised access may also happen to companies by perpetrators for several kinds of purposes

These may include unethical profit gain, ransom attack,[38] phishing,[39] spoofing,[40] money laundering,[41] etc. Unauthorised access to data may also be carried out to malign the reputation of the company. Consider the cases of using the coned email IDs and databases of customers or prospective customers whose data may have been collected by the companies for future business purposes: hackers may reach out to other ordinary individuals with such information for job scams,[42] or for phishing purposes. Consider cases of hacking attacks to LinkedIn in 2012 where several millions of passwords of LinkedIn customers were hacked and compromised.[43] Similarly, in 2019 British Airways also faced a huge hacking attack, whereby the personal data of passengers was leaked by hackers. The company was made liable to pay a large fine by the government.[44] These data may also be used to find out a company's unique business strategies. Apart from the corporate sectors that deal with consumable products, there are several other types of companies in the information communication and digital communication sectors. These may be also associated with other companies and the government for different kinds of third-party services, including manufacture of smart devices, third-party data collection, and data processing who may work on contractual basis with the above-mentioned companies and the government sectors. There are also individual stakeholders, including information technology professionals, students, and ethical hackers who may also be connected with internet service provision as internet content cleaners.[45] All of these stakeholders are reservoirs of huge data, which may include sensitive personal data, images that may be used for biometrical data purposes, financial data, etc. In these companies, as corporate stakeholders may work in different capacities, their legal responsibilities towards their clients may also vary accordingly. Companies and government stakeholders who may have provided contractual obligations to other companies may shift the burden of liability, including civil and criminal liabilities, on their business collaborators for negligence in preventing unauthorised access and unauthorised modification of data. In cases where grave criminal liability may arise, the corporate veil may be lifted by legal stakeholders, including the courts. Key stakeholders in the company may also be made liable for negligence in their roles as representatives of the company, both by the company and by the criminal justice machinery. It is for this very reason that many key representatives of social media companies, giant tech. companies, etc., may have had to resign, or may have had to assume responsibility for criminal charges for the infringement of data privacy of large groups of civilians.[46]

Ordinary individuals are considered the most vulnerable victims of unauthorised access to device and data. The COVID-19 pandemic spread rapidly from China to Europe, other Asian countries the Americas, and Australia. Governments started restricting physical movement because the pandemic spread from human-to-human interaction. By March 2020, the majority of the countries saw lockdowns for indefinite periods that were backed by government orders. Industrial and financial growth became minimal due to the lack of physical commercial activities. However, internet activities grew tremendously during this time. Cyber-crimes also increased during this time. unauthorised access or hacking being the most common expression during this time.[47] The personal data may be unauthorizedly accessed and misused for specific purposes and that may include economic offences, gratification of revenge, sexual gratification, etc.[48] Various forms of unauthorised access schemes were devised, including ransom attacks, romance scams,[49] advance fee scams,[50] job or lottery scams, matrimonial frauds,[51] banking frauds, and hacking of sensitive personal data—including health data, banking data, or even data related to the internet of things—causing financial as well as reputational damage to the victims. Often data owners (in cases of victimisation by way of unauthorised access) may be blamed for not taking proper security measures to protect their devices, data, etc. In such cases, they may have to go through revictimisation when the web companies and corporate bodies processing the data, or stringing the data, refuse to accept their liability for any sort of security breach. Consider the cases of banking frauds: banks may shift the liability to the original data owners for giving away their sensitive personal information in spite of awareness shared by the concerned stakeholders. Women, children, and senior citizens are often blamed for their ignorance for updating the security measures of their data. Young adults are targeted for their documented profiles on social media platforms, which may attract predators.[52]

Cyber espionage

Cyber espionage is another activity that may harm both government as well as corporate entities. In the case of government, cyber espionage may be directly linked with cyber warfare, accessing and using confidential data for the benefit of enemy parties for causing disruption in governance of the country and attacking the information technology, military, and government infrastructure of the country. In the case of attack on corporations, cyber espionage may be directly linked with gaining access to business strategy, trade secrets, etc., for the benefit of competitors in the market, hampering the economic growth of the company, attacking the client database, etc.[53] As such, cyber espionage may be construed from the perspectives of cyber warfare as well as from the perspectives of economic cyber espionage.[54] Cyber espionage may be the next stage of hacking and cracking whereby the victim's cyberinfrastructure may be infected with malicious software that would let the perpetrators know about confidential secrets and would also enable the latter to predict the future activities of the former by way of human and artificial intelligence. Governments may be particularly vulnerable because information regarding the

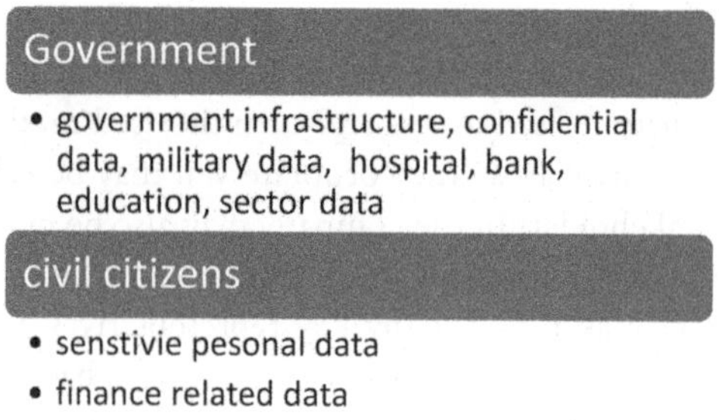

20 Patterns of cyber victimisation

> **Government**
> - government infrastructure, confidential data, military data, hospital, bank, education, sector data
>
> **civil citizens**
> - senstivie pesonal data
> - finance related data

FIGURE 2.2 Effect of cyber espionage on nation states

civil governance, military intelligentsia, etc., may be leaked to other parties in order to cause widespread disruption. Cyber espionage may be carried out by various means, and not just by infecting the computer infrastructure by viruses: image capturing and information collection by use of drones[55] and unauthorised surveillance by use of satellites, etc., may be some ways of conducting cyberspying or espionage. Enemy states, or even terror organisations, may have their own cyber army which may be comprised of hackers who would be commissioned to commit the acts of cyber espionage. The *Tallinn Manual* of 2013 suggests that in the absence of any specific international law/policy or guidelines, laws related to warfare and compensation for war may be applied for acts of cyber espionage, attempts for cyber espionage, and for the consequences of cyber espionage which may not be limited to damage to computer and computer network infrastructure, data privacy, and confidentiality, etc., but which may also cause damage to the human society as a whole.[56] The effect of cyber espionage especially on nation states may be explained through the following flow chart (Figure 2.2):

As may be seen from the above flow chart, cyber espionage may also affect sensitive personal data, including the finance-related data of the civil body as a whole. The purpose of the perpetrators may extend to causing widespread disruption of public services and causing internal as well as external warlike situations.[57] The spying activities may lead to providing information to the enemy parties, who would not only gain information about the secret data, but who might also then proceed to endanger public safety, including affecting the financial database of the citizens and matters concerning interstate commerce as well.

For companies, the act of cyber espionage may be carried out specifically to access trade secrets and damage the reputation of the victim company in the market. Unlike nation states, cyber espionage directed towards companies may be mostly carried out by infecting the computers with malicious softwares, DoS and DDoS, etc. External spywares like drones or satellites may not be used as much as in the case of attacking nation states. However, the extent of damage that may be inflicted may be enormous, as this may necessarily include economic espionage. Several companies also act as data repositories for the sensitive personal data of their customers, irrespective of jurisdiction where the company may be registered. In such cases, cyber espionage may even lead to graver legal problems for the victim company as the said company may have to face multiple liabilities, according to the laws of different jurisdictions. Even though most companies generally indicate their preferred jurisdiction for legal responsibilities and court cases, customers based in different jurisdictions may avail themselves of their own domestic laws in certain situations for compensation for data breach, depending on the criteria of the effect test[58] or long arm test,[59] etc.

Unauthorised access, cyber espionage, etc., may also lead to cyberterrorism. This is not synonymous with cyber warfare, even though many may construe the two concepts as overlapping.

Cyberterrorism is necessarily be done by terror outfits rather than nation states.[60] The modus operandi may be the same in both cases.

Cyber-crime victimisation by way of infringement of intellectual properties

Companies may face victimisation due to copyright and trademark-related criminal activities, cybersquatting, data theft, etc. Digital piracy targeting protected works, including songs, films, and other entertainment-related content is the most common form of victimisation, often targeting companies engaged in distribution, production, and creation of content.[61] In such cases, both the creator (individual) and the distributor/producer (the company) of the content may suffer copyright infringement-related victimisation. Some research has shown that rapid internet penetration into the society at large caused huge losses in the entertainment industry, heavily dependent as it was on the unique distribution method of films and songs.[62] Domain name dispute-related issues, including cybersquatting, are another form of crime victimisation that has reportedly affected several companies in the recent past. Cybersquatting can be explained as an "internet version of a land grab."[63] Curtin (2010) further explains cybersquatting as "...... scams intended to bring Internet users to competitors' sites so that the domain name owners make a profit off of the Internet user's mistake."[64] The Internet Corp. For Assigned Names And Numbers (ICANN), Uniform Domain-Name Dispute-Resolution Policy (1999) in clause 4 (b) indicates the patterns for victimizing a company by registration and use of a domain name in bad faith. These include the following:

i circumstances indicating that you have registered or you have acquired the domain name primarily for the purpose of selling, renting, or otherwise transferring the domain name registration to the complainant who is the owner of the trademark or service mark or to a competitor of that complainant, for valuable consideration in excess of your documented out-of-pocket costs directly related to the domain name; or

ii you have registered the domain name in order to prevent the owner of the trademark or service mark from reflecting the mark in a corresponding domain name, provided that you have engaged in a pattern of such conduct; or

iii you have registered the domain name primarily for the purpose of disrupting the business of a competitor; or

iv by using the domain name, you have intentionally attempted to attract, for commercial gain, Internet users to your web site or other on-line location, by creating a likelihood of confusion with the complainant's mark as to the source, sponsorship, affiliation, or endorsement of your web site or location or of a product or service on your web site or location.[65]

Even though the United States provides some protective measures through the *Anticybersquatting Consumer Protection Act* (1999), not many countries have developed such preventive legislations. However, the highest accorded crime targeting companies and business establishments irrespective of their nature, had remained to be unauthorised access and data theft, which had in turn provided huge illegal monetary profit for hackers and terrorist organisations.

Copyright violation for still and audio-visual images has been considered a significant offence against individual performers, including actors and other individuals. This may not always be related to the films in which an actor has worked, or a musical album that has been created by a singer, or books written by authors. Celebrities, including movie stars, athletes, politicians, and internet celebrities may have a huge fan following. These fans may breach the copyrights of the

22 Patterns of cyber victimisation

former by stealing their personal pictures and/or audio-visual clippings for making mashed up content. Such photographs, images, or audio-visual content may also be used to impersonate ordinary individuals.[66]

Hate and misogynist speech on cyberspace

The virtual environment is engineered to enable users to speak and express their feelings by words, audio-visual content, and by images of various kinds. This right to speech has been expanded to such an extent that it has been misused by many users of cyberspace to create harm to others, including minority communities, women, and people belonging to LGBTQ categories, children, etc. Often this has led to online extremism and the fuelling of terrorism.[67] The consequences of such misuse of the right to speech have also been seen in cases of cyber-bullying, trolling, and reputation damage to individuals, especially women. Online racial abuse has taken a huge toll on Asians, Africans, etc., who may have immigrated to Europe, Australia or the United States for a better living. Research on online speech has shown that people belonging to various kinds of professions, including celebrities may be affected by such speech. Intentional hate speech or misogynist speech may even damage the reputation of the victims to such an extent that it may become difficult for the victim to repair the damage within a short span of time.[68] It may directly affect the victim's prospects in the job market or prospects for marital relationships. Even though cyberbullying has been considered an independent form of speech offence, I strongly argue that it must be considered within the parameters of online hate speech. Bullying may be interpersonal and may be targeted to a specific group but considering the inherent nature of cyberbullying, it may very well be accommodated within the meaning of hate speech. Trolling, on the other hand, rather than a form of hate speech, signifies a vicious wish to attract attention to his or her own opinion. But this is not a form of free speech either, especially when the consequences of such trolling may lead to wider harm to the victim.[69] Often it has been reported that the companies providing platforms for such speech and expression are liable for escalating the level of victimization, as they have their own policies to control and regulate contents.[70] Non-US researchers have indicated that as most of the web companies are hosted in the United States, they have followed US laws for speech and expression, which are extremely broad.[71] While this is partly true, several US-based researchers have also indicated that the wider scope of free speech rights has caused victimisation to people who may be living within a US jurisdiction.[72] Web companies are, however, being repeatedly told by governments of different countries to consider restrictive speech laws of different countries for content moderation on their platforms. Several countries have also reportedly prohibited operation of certain web companies in their jurisdiction, as the latter had repeatedly failed to control content, including speech that may have violated the former's moral and legal speech criteria.

Privacy violation-related victimisation for ordinary individuals

The central point of cyber victimisation for individuals may be privacy. Privacy, again should not be understood only within the meaning of data privacy emphasised by stakeholders, such as laid out by the European Union General Data Protection Regulations. The concept of privacy may include data privacy, as well as bodily privacy. Let me now explain why data privacy has been given such significance in the discussions on cyber-crime victimisations of individuals. Privacy violation may relate to different types of cyber-crime victimisation. This can be explained through the following flow chart (Figure 2.3):

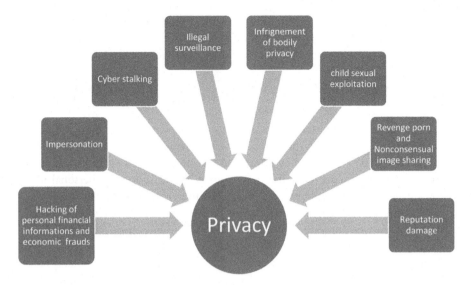

FIGURE 2.3 Privacy violations in different kinds of cyber-crimes targeting individuals

Financial frauds and hacking

When we speak about cyber-crimes against ordinary individuals, the first thought that comes into our mind is economic fraud. Since the growth of e-commerce, the reliance on online transactions, online banking, and e wallets has skyrocketed. The highest surge was seen during the COVID-19 lockdown in 2020.[73] Presently, no country may deny the fact that government and privatised banks, companies, and government institutions, including the courts, encourage citizens to perform online transactions. The occasions for online transactions are countless and include depositing money for receiving licenses, paying bills for children's education and hospital costs, and paying fines and depositing amounts for compensation in matters of the restitution of justice. Four parties are engaged in such transactions: the payee, the payer, the bank, and the payment gate agents. While many may think that the payee (especially in the case where it is a company) may try to remember the payment details and may misuse such details, including the bank and bankcard details, in fact payment gate agents may be secret agents hired to record transaction and banking details. There is a human brain behind every machine; hence, the role of such payment agents or corporate payees in leaking out bank details of customers to organised criminal gangs for the purpose of criminal activities, including ransomware attacks etc, may not be ruled out. While this may be a type of economic fraud, ordinary individuals irrespective of gender may be targeted by romance scams, job scams, lottery scams, gift scams, or advance fee scams, and phishing attacks based on such ploys as seeking help as an individual stuck in a foreign land with no money, etc. In most of these scam cases, victims are often blamed for their greed in wishing to obtain quick money and ignorance of safety alerts that may have been shared by the government and non-government organisations. Several studies have shown that victims of economic frauds may often be youth in need of a job or looking for quick money;[74] The victim's profile may also include women. While young women are most often victims of sexual offences, women aged 30 and above, especially widows, single women, and divorcees with young children, may fall victim to romance scams, as they seek decent and compassionate male partners who may not only provide financial security to them, but may also provide love and affection to them and their children. Senior citizens, irrespective of their gender, are the most susceptible victims of economic fraud. Retired pensioners and other senior citizens who may not be familiar

Patterns of cyber victimisation

with digital culture may give out banking details to the perpetrators over the phone or at ATM kiosks while trusting the latter to be helpful.[75] The above-mentioned financial frauds may also be done by way of hacking the personal data and devices of the victims.[76]

Impersonation

In the age of social media, impersonation has been considered one of the most common crimes targeting women and children.[77] Perpetrators may either create impersonating profiles to groom the victims for the purpose of sexual exploitation or economic fraud or may impersonate genuine profiles by unauthorisedly accessing such profiles and misusing the personal identifiable information of the original profile owners. Ordinary individuals, including women and adolescents, may also be harassed by the creation of profiles that may impersonate them to their friends and acquaintances. Impersonation may be considered one the most significant tools for interpersonal victimisation.

Cyberstalking

Women and girls are considered the most vulnerable victims of cyberstalking, which involves monitoring online as well as real life activities of the victims. Cyberstalking involves privacy violation. The stalker generally tries to monitor the activities of the victims by hacking into personal devices, email IDs or social media profiles of the victim/s or by engaging a proxy stalker to monitor the victim. The ultimate aim of the stalker is to make the victim feel threatened and thus surrender to the stalker's demands. Cyberstalking may result in the publication of revenge porn materials or hacking of personal information of the victim or even physical attacks on the victim.[78]

Illegal surveillance

Post the 9/11 Twin Tower attack, governments in many countries became extremely vigilant about 'suspicious' activities of individuals that might lead to terrorism and/or civil unrest. The Arab Spring in early 2010 was one of the first social media uprisings against bad governance.[79] This led to civil unrest in several Middle Eastern countries; later, the bulk of the information generated on internet platforms had been allegedly used by terror organisations to create widespread attacks on governments and civil society members. After the Arab Spring several separatist groups created their own web pages to express opinions. Social media platforms have also been widely used for communicating with people who share common opinions. All these were possible because of extremely wide freedom of speech and expression laws in the United States. Websites hosted in the United States enjoyed the freedom to receive third-party immunity for the content posted by users. This created political chaos. Several states created their own legal mechanisms to decrypt the private communication of people over the internet whenever the former felt such an act was necessary for the safety of the nation.[80] Such acts of the government had curtailed freedom of speech to a large extent. But this created a huge barrier to the privacy rights of ordinary individuals. Privacy right activists have raised their voices against unwanted and illegal surveillance tools used by government agencies. On numerous occasions courts have indicated that facial recognition tools used by the police as a surveillance mechanism are illegal and violative of privacy rights.[81]

Infringement of bodily privacy

Unauthorised access to data, devices, networks, or hacking may be directly connected with the infringement upon bodily privacy. Data privacy related to hospital data, online clothing and shoe purchases, bodily care-related products and services commuting services like Uber, and even online tickets for holidays, hotel bookings, etc may be documented by system-generated mechanisms. These may often be misused when the customer data is leaked or the cyberinfrastructure of the company or the customer's devices and data are hacked. The information thus achieved may be used for a wide ranges of purposes: online sex racketing,[82] porn contents for the porn markets,[83] ransom attacks, attacks on physical space for robbery or for sexual crimes on the basis of the information so gathered,[84] and for interpersonal criminal activities, including revenge porn.[85] Bodily privacy may also be infringed upon by way spy cameras that may be activated through the internet of things, including smart toys and other camera-enabled gadgets used for domestic purposes.[86]

Child online sexual exploitation

Privacy violation is an inherent factor in child online sexual exploitation cases.[87] The presence of adolescents in cyberspace is increasing rapidly. There is also a huge increase in online activities for adolescents: numerous online games have been created by app developers. The COVID-19 pandemic period (spanning from March 2020 until 2021 when this book was being written) has also seen an increase in online classes for children. Parents had to provide almost unlimited access to the internet for children because the need to engage in their work, required their use of the internet as a pacifier. All these factors have increased the risk of privacy infringement of children to a great degree.[88] Apart from this, there are numerous organised groups that have been running online child trafficking rackets on the basis of images of children available on cyberspace.[89] It has been often alleged that such images and information have been made available by the parents and children themselves because of their habits of oversharing of information on various web platforms, including social media sites like Instagram.

Revenge porn and non-consensual image sharing

The terms revenge porn and non-consensual image sharing may sound synonymous. But in reality, these are different. Both attack privacy of the victims (primarily women). However, in the case of revenge porn, the perpetrator may necessarily share personal images of the victim as porn content to gratify personal anger and revenge.[90] Because such sharing of images does not include the consent of the owner of the image or the personal identifiable data, it is also termed as non-consensual image sharing.[91] But all non-consensual image sharing cases are not revenge porn. In many instances, images of ordinary individuals have been captured randomly and shared on internet platforms. Again, personal photographs or voyeur images of celebrities may be shared on internet platforms without proper consent for profit making.[92] Such forms of privacy violations may be carried out in numerous ways, including hacking into the personal profiles of celebrities or ordinary individuals whose images may be 'stolen' from their profiles. Non-consensual image sharing may also include capturing images of the targeted individual/s by using mobile phone cameras, spy cameras, or other sophisticated cameras, including drones, and sharing or selling such images on internet platforms for profit. It is unfortunate to note that there has been a steep increase in the use of such mechanisms for capturing images of private individuals, only to harass them later.

26 Patterns of cyber victimisation

Reputation damage

Privacy violations by way of non-consensual image capturing and sharing, revenge porn, hacking, doxing (which involves data mining of the victim and sharing the same to cause shame and embarrassment in public), etc., may damage the reputation of the victim in cyberspace as well as in real life. Most of the above-mentioned privacy breaches are done by the perpetrators (especially in interpersonal criminal activities) to cause reputation damage to the victim. Consider the cases of revenge porn: when the perpetrator publishes such content on the internet, it may directly impact he reputation of the victim in the job market.[93] Hate speech or doxing may also impact the social reputation of the victim and may infringe upon the physical security of the victim as well.[94]

2.2 Profiling Victims of Cyber-Crimes

Patterns of cyber victimisation and the impact of the same may best be understood by profiling the victims. Several research reports have showed different types of statistics for victims and cyber victimisations. However, the cyber-crime reports from the United Kingdom,[95] Australia,[96] the United States,[97] and India[98] until 2020 suggest that governments were victimised by malicious virus attacks. Most of the countries encountered attacks on their confidential data. The attackers had been organised gangs, and the major motive had been unethical gain by ransom attacks. As has been discussed above, governments are susceptible to cyberterrorism, espionage and cyber warfare. But as the existing data may also show, governments are increasingly becoming victims of malicious virus attacks and ransom attacks as well. Research has also shown that countries with weak cyber-crime legislation may become victims of a number of organised cyber-crimes, including attacks on the confidential public health data, financial data, etc. African countries are considered to be more vulnerable in this regard.[99] Companies, on the other hand, are also vulnerable victims of ransomware. They may also be victimised by copyright and trademark infringements by individual perpetrators or organised criminal gangs. Companies are vulnerable to becoming victimized by impersonation fraud as well, especially in cases of using the company logo or spoofing the company email ID, websites, and the like for job scams. Small-scale companies with less financial means may be the most vulnerable victims, as they may not be able to recover the financial loss and damage to their reputation as quickly as bigger companies. The following flow chart may explain the profile of the State and companies as victims (Figure 2.4):

Profiling of ordinary individuals, including men, women, and children may be different than the first two categories (the State and companies) discussed above.

Reports have almost unanimously suggested that women are the most vulnerable victims of cybersexual offences Reports from the United Kingdom, the United States, and Australia have also shown that women are increasingly becoming victims of financial fraud. Women from the age group of 30 and above may fall victim to online fraud, including romance fraud. Women are also the most chosen targets for hate speech and misogynist bullying. Women bloggers, online content creators, and entrepreneurs are the most victimised in this regard. The perpetrators may be both males and females. The above-mentioned reports have further suggested that women and men suffered from e-commerce-related frauds almost in equal ratio: this includes non-delivery of goods and services, non-delivery of refunds, etc. It has also been observed that women are increasingly becoming victims of online sexual harassment by their supervisors and male colleagues.[100] Women from non-Western countries are also becoming victims of sextortion by their male colleagues, online acquaintances, and boyfriends.[101] But lack of awareness, fear of

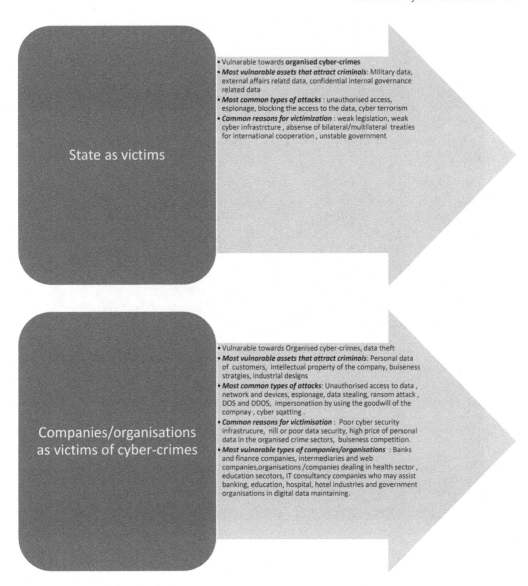

FIGURE 2.4 Profile of state and companies as victims

social taboos, and lack of digital empowerment may prevent such women from accessing justice to the same extent as their counterparts in Western countries.[102] The majority of research has suggested that men are perpetrators of online sexual offences. But recent studies have also shown that men in the age group of 25 and above are increasingly becoming victims of sextortion.[103] The perpetrators may be organised gangs.[104] It is pertinent to note here that the COVID-19 pandemic period has led many women to open their YouTube channels to showcase their talents and earn revenue. Such women YouTubers who create content on lifestyle may also attract victimisation by way of cyberstalking, non-consensual image sharing, and defamation. The majority of the reports (as discussed above) have shown that children under 18 years of age are vulnerable targets for sexual exploitation. Children from socio-economically advantaged classes may be victimised by online bullying from their peers. Most children who may lack proper monitoring of their internet activities at home and at school may become addicted to online games and/or

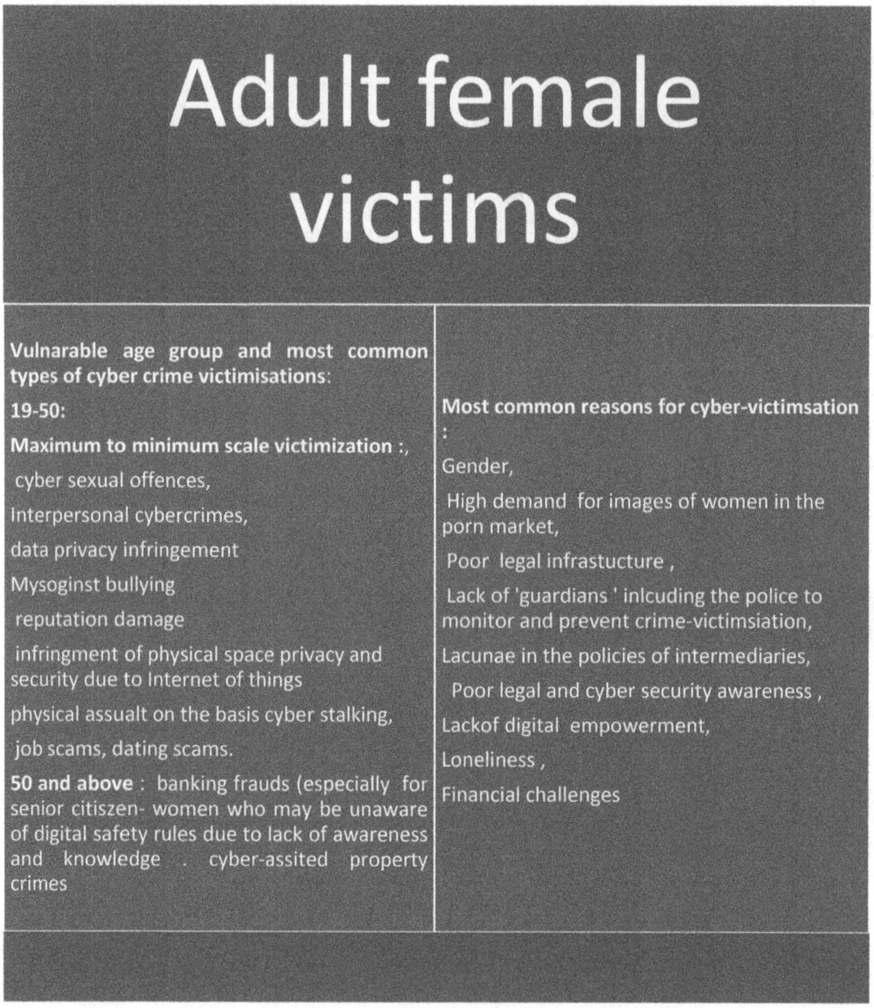

28 Patterns of cyber victimisation

Adult female victims

Vulnarable age group and most common types of cyber crime victimisations: **19-50:** **Maximum to minimum scale victimization :,** cyber sexual offences, Interpersonal cybercrimes, data privacy infringement Mysoginst bullying reputation damage infringment of physical space privacy and security due to Internet of things physical assualt on the basis cyber stalking, job scams, dating scams. **50 and above** : banking frauds (especially for senior citiszen- women who may be unaware of digital safety rules due to lack of awareness and knowledge . cyber-assited property crimes	**Most common reasons for cyber-victimsation :** Gender, High demand for images of women in the porn market, Poor legal infrastucture , Lack of 'guardians ' inlcuding the police to monitor and prevent crime-victimsiation, Lacunae in the policies of intermediaries, Poor legal and cyber security awareness , Lackof digital empowerment, Loneliness , Financial challenges

FIGURE 2.5 Profiling of female victims of cyber-crimes

porn contents. Due to their lack of maturity, children may also avail irrational coping mechanisms to resist bullies or remove unwanted content that may victimise them.[105] Further, due to poverty, many adolescents and young adults particularly in countries like Nigeria, India, Pakistan, Bangladesh, and Iraq, more broadly in Latin America, Middle Eastern countries, and Eastern European countries may become perpetrators themselves. They may commit economic fraud including 419 scams. Some children may even consider joining the terror organisations through the online recruiters, without understanding the consequences of the same. Women in general may attract victimisation in cyberspace due to their gender and the ever-growing internet porn industry, where women of all ages may be considered as consumable porn products. This profiling may be explained through the following flow chart (Figures 2.5, 2.6, and 2.7):

It is sad to note that several countries across the globe engage in victim blaming of both female and male victims of cyber-crime, irrespective of their age. Male victims may prefer not to cooperate with the criminal justice machinery if they encounter victim blaming. Similarly, female victims may not prefer to report crimes of victimisation, likewise fearing victim blaming.

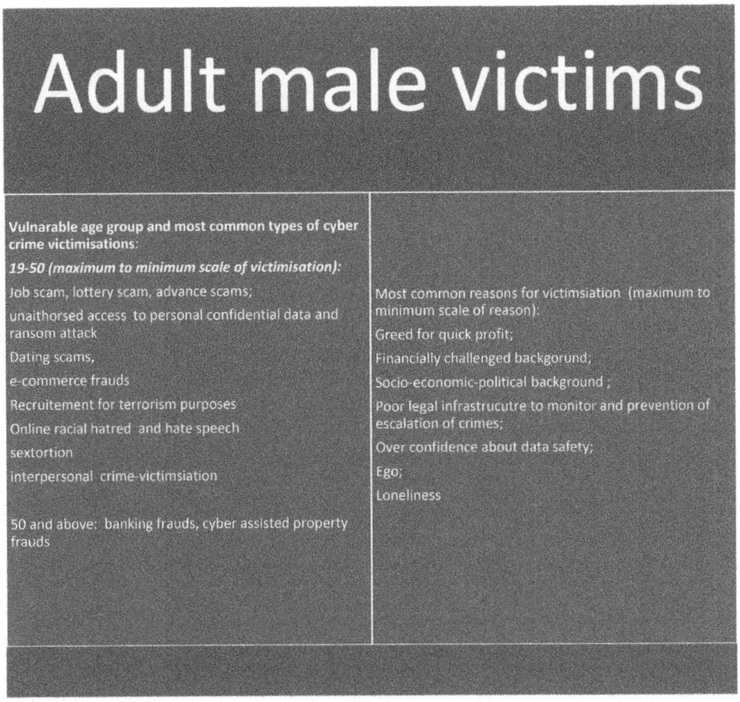

Adult male victims

Vulnarable age group and most common types of cyber crime victimisations:

19-50 (maximum to minimum scale of victimisation):

Job scam, lottery scam, advance scams;

unaithorsed access to personal confidential data and ransom attack

Dating scams,

e-commerce frauds

Recruitement for terrorism purposes

Online racial hatred and hate speech

sextortion

interpersonal crime-victimsiation

50 and above: banking frauds, cyber assisted property frauds

Most common reasons for victimsiation (maximum to minimum scale of reason):

Greed for quick profit;

Financially challenged backgorund;

Socio-economic-political background ;

Poor legal infrastrucutre to monitor and prevention of escalation of crimes;

Over confidence about data safety;

Ego;

Loneliness

FIGURE 2.6 Profiling of male victims of cyber-crimes

Children as victims

Most common reasons for victimization:

Unmonitored use of cyber space;

inquisitiveness;

Peer influence;

Restrictions in outdoor activities;

Over sharing of personal information;

Lonliness;

Demand of child sexual contents in the porn market;

Lack of awareness regarding reporting agencies

Greed for quick profit

Poor legal infrastruture

Most vulnarable age and most common types of victimsiation

(maximum to minimum scale of victimization) :

8–18 :

Sexual offences, grooming and impersonation

Hacking of profiles and confidential data

Sextortions

Cyber bullying

Interpersonal victimsiation

Dating scams

FIGURE 2.7 Profiling of children as victims of cyber-crimes

30 Patterns of cyber victimisation

Notes

1 Brenner, S.W. (2007). History of computer crime. In K. de Leeuw and J. Bergstra (Eds.), *The history of information security* (pp. 705–721). Oxford: Elsevier Science BV.

2 Lessig L. *The Laws of cyber space.*(1998). https://cyber.harvard.edu/works/lessig/laws_cyberspace.pdf

3 See Malware attacks: What you need to know. (2019). Available at https://us.norton.com/internetsecurity-malware-malware-101-how-do-i-get-malware-complex-attacks.html#:~:text=A%20malware%20attack%20is%20when,%2C%20ransomware%2C%20and%20Trojan%20horses

4 See Title 1 of the *Convention on cybercrime*, 2001. Available at https://rm.coe.int/1680081561. Accessed on 22.01.21.

5 See in Title 2 in Ibid.

6 See in Title 3 in Ibid.

7 See in Title 4 in Ibid.

8 More information is available at https://www.coe.int/en/web/conventions/full-list/-/conventions/treaty/189. Accessed on 20.01.2021.

9 More information is available at https://www.coe.int/en/web/conventions/full-list/-/conventions/treaty/196. Accessed on 21.01.2021.

10 More information is available at https://www.coe.int/en/web/conventions/full-list/-/conventions/treaty/201. Accessed on 21.01.2021.

11 For more information, see *EU General Data Protection Regulation*. (2016). Available at https://gdpr-info.eu/ Accessed on 21.01.2021.

12 Kshetri, N. (2005). Pattern of global cyber war and crime: A conceptual framework. *Journal of International Management*, 11(4), 541–562.

13 Wall, D. (2007). *Cybercrime: The transformation of crime in the information age* (Vol. 4). Polity.

14 Halder, D., & Jaishankar, K. (2016). *Cyber crimes against women in India*. New Delhi: SAGE Publications.

15 Denning, D. (2000). "Cyberterrorism", Testimony before the Special Oversight Panel of Terrorism Committee on Armed Services, US House of Representatives, 23 May 2000. Available at http://www.cs.georgetown.edu/~denning/infosec/cyberter ror.html. Accessed on 12.12.2020.

16 Kenney, M. (2015). Cyberterrorism in a post-stuxnet world. *Orbis*, 59(1), 111–128.

17 See Denning, D. (2007). A view of cyberterrorism five years later. In K. Himma (Ed.), *Readings in Internet security: Hacking, counterhacking, and society* (pp. 123–40). Boston: Jones & Barlette Publishers; Ilardi, G. J. (2009). The 9/11 attacks—a study of Al Qaeda's use of intelligence and counterintelligence. *Studies in Conflict & Terrorism*, 32(3), 171–187.

18 Weissbrodt, D. (2013). Cyber-conflict, cyber-crime, and cyber-espionage. *Minnesorta Journal of International Law*, 22, 347 (2013). Available at https://scholarship.law.umn.edu/faculty_articles/223

19 Giantas, D., & Stergiou, D. (2018). *From terrorism to cyber-terrorism: The case of ISIS*. Available at SSRN 3135927; Kenney, M. (2015). Cyber-terrorism in a post-stuxnet world. *Orbis*, 59(1), 111–128.

20 Ibid.

21 Ibid.

22 For more, see Rudner, M. (2017). "Electronic Jihad": The Internet as Al Qaeda's catalyst for global terror. *Studies in Conflict & Terrorism*, 40(1), 10–23.; Denning, D. E. (2011). Whither cyber terror? 10 years after September 11. In *A Social Science Research Council Essay Forum*. (2011). Available at http://essays. ssrc. org/10yearsafter911/whither-cyber-terror/. Accessed on 23.04.2012.

23 Weissbrodt, D. (2013). Cyber-conflict, cyber-crime, and cyber-espionage. *Minnesota Journal of International Law, 22*, 347 (2013). Available at https://scholarship.law.umn.edu/faculty_articles/223

24 Kshetri, N. (2005). Pattern of global cyber war and crime: A conceptual framework. *Journal of International Management*, 11(4), 541–562.

25 Trautman, L.J., & Ormerod, P.C. (2018). Wannacry, ransomware, and the emerging threat to corporations. *Tennessee Law Review*, 86, 503.

26 Sinrod, E.J. & Reilly, W.P. (2000). Cyber-crimes: A practical approach to the application of federal computer crime laws. *Santa Clara High Tech. Law Journal*, 16,. Available at http://digitalcommons.law.scu.edu/chtlj/vol16/iss2/1

27 Ibid.

28 Ibid.

29 See S.18 USC § 1030(e)(2).

30 Hayes, C. R. (2016). Maritime cybersecurity: the future of national security (Doctoral dissertation, Monterey, California: Naval Postgraduate School).

31 See 18 U.S. Code § 1030—Fraud and related activity in connection with computers which says as follows: Whoever—

1. having knowingly accessed a computer without authorization or exceeding authorized access, and by means of such conduct having obtained information that has been determined by the United States Government pursuant to an Executive order or statute to require protection against unauthorized disclosure for reasons of national defense or foreign relations, or any restricted data, as defined in paragraph y. of section 11 of the *Atomic Energy Act* of 1954, with reason to believe that such information so obtained could be used to the injury of the United States, or to the advantage of any foreign nation willfully communicates, delivers, transmits, or causes to be communicated, delivered, or transmitted, or attempts to communicate, deliver, transmit or cause to be communicated, delivered, or transmitted the same to any person not entitled to receive it, or willfully retains the same and fails to deliver it to the officer or employee of the United States entitled to receive it;
2. intentionally accesses a computer without authorization or exceeds authorized access, and thereby obtains—

   A. information contained in a financial record of a financial institution, or of a card issuer as defined in section 1602(n) [1] of title 15, or contained in a file of a consumer reporting agency on a consumer, as such terms are defined in the *Fair Credit Reporting Act* (15 U.S.C. 1681 et seq.);
   B. information from any department or agency of the United States; or
   C. information from any protected computer;

3. intentionally, without authorization to access any nonpublic computer of a department or agency of the United States, accesses such a computer of that department or agency that is exclusively for the use of the Government of the United States or, in the case of a computer not exclusively for such use, is used by or for the Government of the United States and such conduct affects that use by or for the Government of the United States;
4. knowingly and with intent to defraud, accesses a protected computer without authorization, or exceeds authorized access, and by means of such conduct furthers the intended fraud and obtains anything of value, unless the object of the fraud and the thing obtained consists only of the use of the computer and the value of such use is not more than $5,000 in any 1-year period;
5.

   A. knowingly causes the transmission of a program, information, code, or command, and as a result of such conduct, intentionally causes damage without authorization, to a protected computer;
   B. intentionally accesses a protected computer without authorization, and as a result of such conduct, recklessly causes damage; or
   C. intentionally accesses a protected computer without authorization, and as a result of such conduct, causes damage and loss. [2]

6. knowingly and with intent to defraud traffics (as defined in section 1029) in any password or similar information through which a computer may be accessed without authorization, if—

   A. such trafficking affects interstate or foreign commerce; or
   B. such computer is used by or for the Government of the United States; [3]

7. with intent to extort from any person any money or other thing of value, transmits in interstate or foreign commerce any communication containing any—

   A. threat to cause damage to a protected computer;
   B. threat to obtain information from a protected computer without authorization or in excess of authorization or to impair the confidentiality of information obtained from a protected computer without authorization or by exceeding authorized access; or
   C. demand or request for money or other thing of value in relation to damage to a protected computer, where such damage was caused to facilitate the extortion;

   shall be punished as provided in subsection (c) of this section.

32 Patterns of cyber victimisation

32 For example, see S.1 of *Computer Misuse Act*, 1990 which says as follows:

Unauthorised access to computer material.

1. A person is guilty of an offence if—

    a. he causes a computer to perform any function with intent to secure access to any program or data held in any computer [F1, or to enable any such access to be secured];
    b. the access he intends to secure [F2, or to enable to be secured,] is unauthorised; and
    c. he knows at the time when he causes the computer to perform the function that that is the case.

2. The intent a person has to have to commit an offence under this section need not be directed at—

    a. any particular program or data;
    b. a program or data of any particular kind; or
    c. a program or data held in any particular compute

33 See S.3ZA of the *Computer Misuse Act*, 1990 which says as follows:

Unauthorised acts causing, or creating risk of, serious damage

1. A person is guilty of an offence if—

    a. the person does any unauthorised act in relation to a computer;
    b. at the time of doing the act the person knows that it is unauthorised;
    c. the act causes, or creates a significant risk of, serious damage of a material kind; and
    d. the person intends by doing the act to cause serious damage of a material kind or is reckless as to whether such damage is caused.

2. Damage is of a "material kind" for the purposes of this section if it is—

    a. damage to human welfare in any place;
    b. damage to the environment of any place;
    c. damage to the economy of any country; or
    d. damage to the national security of any country.

3. For the purposes of subsection (2)(a) an act causes damage to human welfare only if it causes—

    a. loss to human life;
    b. human illness or injury;
    c. disruption of a supply of money, food, water, energy or fuel;
    d. disruption of a system of communication;
    e. disruption of facilities for transport; or
    f. disruption of services relating to health.

4. It is immaterial for the purposes of subsection (2) whether or not an act causing damage—

    a. does so directly;
    b. is the only or main cause of the damage.

5. In this section—

    a. a reference to doing an act includes a reference to causing an act to be done;
    b. "act" includes a series of acts;
    c. a reference to a country includes a reference to a territory, and to any place in, or part or region of, a country or territory.

6. A person guilty of an offence under this section is (unless subsection (7) applies) liable, on conviction on indictment, to imprisonment for a term not exceeding 14 years, or to a fine, or to both.

7. Where an offence under this section is committed as a result of an act causing or creating a significant risk of—

    a. serious damage to human welfare of the kind mentioned in subsection (3)(a) or (3)(b), or
    b. serious damage to national security, a person guilty of the offence is liable, on conviction on indictment, to imprisonment for life, or to a fine, or to both.

34 For example, consider Part III of the *Computer Misuse Act*, 1990, Singapore, which discusses offences related to unauthorised access to the computer, etc., under Ss. 3–10.

35 See Part 10.7 in the *Cybercrime Act*, 2001 of Australia.

36 See Ss. 183 & 184 of the *Criminal Code*, Canada. Also see Ss.7 & 8 of the *Federal Privacy Act* (1982) of Canada.

37 S.43 with S.66 and 65 of the *Information Technology Act*, 2000 (amended in 2008) addresses unauthorised access to the computer, computer networking data, etc.

38 A ransom attack may include the application of some sort of malware and capturing the data by the perpetrators. Victims may be blocked from accessing the said data unless they are paying a huge ransom as demanded by the perpetrators. Victims may also be threatened that such private data may be published for public viewing unless they pay the perpetrators in response to the latters' demands. (Young, A., & Yung, M. (1996). Cryptovirology: extortion-based security threats and countermeasures. *IEEE Symposium on Security and Privacy*. pp. 129–140. doi:10.1109/SECPRI.1996.502676. ISBN: 0-8186-7417-2.

39 Google in their policy and support system explains a phishing attack as tricking the victim to share his/her personal data. (See https://support.google.com/websearch/answer/106318?hl=en. Accessed on 12.12.2020.)

40 Spoofing happens when the perpetrator successfully impersonates a business identity or a personal identity and extracts personal information from the victims through the said impersonated identity. (For more information, see https://www.forcepoint.com/cyber-edu/spoofing#:~:text=Spoofing%20is%20the%20act%20of,Name%20System%20(DNS)%20server.)

41 Levi, M., & Reuter, P. (2006). Money laundering. *Crime and Justice*, 34(1), 289–375.

42 le Roy, G. (2007). The great corporate job scam: Money for nothing. *Race, Poverty & the Environment*, 14(1), 9–12.

43 See Andy, B. (2017). LinkedIn 2012 hack: What you need to know. Available at https://www.ncsc.gov.uk/blog-post/linkedin-2012-hack-what-you-need-know on 28-06-2017. Accessed on 21.12.2020.

44 See British Airways faces record £183m fine for data breach. Available at https://www.bbc.com/news/business-48905907. Accessed on 08.07.2019.

45 For discussion of the film documentary on this topic, see Bogle, A. The Cleaners: Meet the hidden people who clean up the worst of the internet.(2018). *ABC Science.* 29 September 2018. Available at https://www.abc.net.au/news/science/2018-09-29/the-cleaners-documentary-social-media-moderation-the-philippines/10300098 on 29-09-2018. Accessed on 21.12.2020.

46 For example, FTC imposes $5 billion penalty and sweeping new privacy restrictions on Facebook. Available at https://www.ftc.gov/news-events/press-releases/2019/07/ftc-imposes-5-billion-penalty-sweeping-new-privacy-restrictions on 24.07.2019. Accessed on 21.12.2020.

47 Lallie, H.S., Shepherd, L.A., Nurse, J R., Erola, A., Epiphaniou, G., Maple, C., & Bellekens, X. (2021). Cyber security in the age of covid-19: A timeline and analysis of cyber-crime and cyber-attacks during the pandemic. *Computers & Security*, *105*, 102248.

48 Halder D., & Jaishankar, K. (2012*). Cyber crime and the victimization of women: Laws, rights, and regulations.* Hershey, PA, USA: IGI Global. ISBN: 978-1-60960-830-9.

49 Such scams are carried out by perpetrators to cheat the victims by posing as lonely bachelors, widowers, etc., to gain their sympathy and then to dupe them financially. Whitty, M.T. (2015). Anatomy of the online dating romance scam. *Security Journal*, 28(4), 443–455.

50 This is a type of notorious Nigerian 419 scam where the victims are tricked by promising them a share in the property of any property owner dying without any successor, or any lottery amount or gift amount which may be released after the payment of an advance by the victim. For a greater understanding on this, see Edelson, E. (2003). The 419 scam: information warfare on the spam front and a proposal for local filtering. *Computers & Security*, *22*(5), 392–401.

51 See in Halder D., & Jaishankar, K (2016.) *Cyber crimes against women in India.* New Delhi: SAGE Publications. ISBN: 9789385985775.

52 Leukfeldt, E.R., & Yar, M. (2016). Applying routine activity theory to cybercrime: A theoretical and empirical analysis. *Deviant Behavior*, *37*(3), 263–280.

53 O'Hara, G. (2010). Cyber-espionage: A growing threat to the American economy. *CommLaw Conspectus*, *19*, 241.

54 Ibid.

55 Herrmann, D. (2019). Cyber espionage and cyber defence. In C. Reuter (Ed.), *Information Technology for Peace and Security* (pp. 83–106). Wiesbaden, Germany: Springer Vieweg.

56 Schmitt, M.N. (Ed.). (2013). *Tallinn manual on the international law applicable to cyber warfare.* Cambridge University Press.

57 Ibid.

58 This is explained in later parts of the book

59 This is explained in later parts of the book.

60 Halder, D. (2011). Information technology act and cyber terrorism: A critical review. In P. Madhava Soma Sundaram, & S. Umarhathab (Eds.), *Cyber crime and digital disorder* (pp. 75–90). Tirunelveli, India: Publication Division, Manonmaniam Sundaranar University.

61 Belleflamme, P. & Peitz, M. Digital Piracy: Theory (October 27, 2010). *CESifo Working Paper Series* No. 3222, Available at SSRN: https://ssrn.com/abstract=1698618

62 Yar, M. (2005). The global 'epidemic' of movie 'piracy': crime-wave or social construction? *Media, Culture & Society*, 27(5), 677–696.

63 *Virtual Works Inc. v. Volkswagen of Am., Inc.*, 238 F.3d 264, 267 (4th Cir. 2001). Also see Curtain, T.J. (2010). The name game: Cybersquatting and trademark infringement on social media websites. *Journal of Law & Policy*, 19. Available at https://brooklynworks.brooklaw.edu/jlp/vol19/iss1/13

64 Curtain, T.J. (2010). The name game: Cybersquatting and trademark infringement on social media websites. *Journal of Law & Policy*, 19. Available at: https://brooklynworks.brooklaw.edu/jlp/vol19/iss1/13

65 See Clause 4(b) in the Internet Corp. For Assigned Names And Numbers (ICANN), Uniform Domain Resolution Policy (1999). Available at https://www.icann.org/resources/pages/policy-2012-02-25-en Accessed on 21.02.2021.

66 Halder D., & Jaishankar K. (2016) Celebrities and cyber crimes: An analysis of the victimization of female film stars on the Internet. *Temida – The Journal on Victimization, Human Rights and Gender*. 19(3-4), 355–372. ISSN: 14506637.

67 Banks, J. (2010). Regulating hate speech online. *International Review of Law, Computers & Technology, 24*(3), 233–239.

68 Citron, D.K. (2014). *Hate crimes in cyberspace*. Harvard University Press.

69 Citron, D.K., & Norton, H. (2011). Intermediaries and hate speech: Fostering digital citizenship for our information age. *Boston University Law Review, 91*, 435.

70 Ibid.

71 Halder D., & Jaishankar, K (2016.) *Cyber crimes against women in India*. New Delhi: SAGE Publications. ISBN: 9789385985775

72 Jane, E.A. (2016). Online misogyny and feminist digilantism. *Continuum, 30*(3), 284–297.

73 Lallie, H.S., Shepherd, L., Nurse, J R., Erola, A., Epiphaniou, G., Maple, C., & Bellekens, X. (2021). Cyber security in the age of covid-19: A timeline and analysis of cybercrime and cyberattacks during the pandemic. *Computers & Security*, 102248.

74 Button, M., Lewis, C., & Tapley, J. (2014). Not a victimless crime: The impact of fraud on individual victims and their families. *Security Journal, 27*(1), 36–54.

75 Li, J.C., Yu, M., Wong, G.T., & Ngan, R.M. (2016). Understanding and preventing financial fraud against older citizens in Chinese society: Results of a focus group study. *International Journal of Offender Therapy and Comparative Criminology, 60*(13), 1509–1531.

76 See the above paragraphs for discussions on this under the title "unauthorised access."

77 Halder, D., & Jaishankar K. (2009). Cyber Socializing and Victimization of Women. *Temida - The Journal on Victimization, Human Rights and Gender,* September 2009, 12(3), 5–26. ISSN: 14506637.

78 Halder D., & Jaishankar, K. (2012). *Cyber Crime and the Victimization of Women: Laws, Rights, and Regulations.* Hershey, PA, USA: IGI Global. ISBN: 978-1-60960-830-9; Pittaro, M.L. (2007). Cyber stalking: An analysis of online harassment and intimidation. *International Journal of Cyber Criminology, 1*(2), 180–197. Ellison, L., & Akdeniz, Y. (1998). Cyber-stalking: the regulation of harassment on the Internet. *Criminal Law Review, 29*, 29–48.

79 Khondker, H.H. (2011). Role of the new media in the Arab Spring. *Globalizations, 8*(5), 675–679.

80 Semitsu, J.P. (2011). From Facebook to mug shot: How the dearth of social networking privacy rights revolutionized online government surveillance. *Pace Law Review, 31*, 291.

81 Winder, D. (2020). Police facial recognition use unlawful—U.K. Court of Appeal makes landmark ruling. Available at https://www.forbes.com/sites/daveywinder/2020/08/12/police-facial-recognition-use-unlawful-uk-court-of-appeal-makes-landmark-ruling/?sh=69414e075e02 on 12-08-2020. Accessed on 13.08.2020.

82 Patella-Rey, P. J. (2018). Beyond privacy: bodily integrity as an alternative framework for understanding non-consensual pornography. *Information, Communication & Society*, 21(5), 786–791.

83 Ibid.

84 Finn, R.L., Wright, D., & Friedewald, M. (2013). Seven types of privacy. In S. Gutwirth, R. Leenes, P. de Hert, & Y. Poullet (Eds.), *European data protection: Coming of age* (pp. 3–32). Springer, Dordrecht.

85 Franks, M.A. (2011). Unwilling avatars: Idealism and discrimination in cyberspace. *Columbia Journal of Gender and Law*, 20, 224.

86 Dabbagh, M., & Rayes, A. (2019). Internet of things: Security and privacy. In A. Rayes, & S. Salam (Eds.), *Internet of things: From hype to reality* (pp. 211–238). Springer, Cham.

87 Seigfried-Spellar, K. C., & Soldino, V. (2020). Child sexual exploitation: Introduction to a global problem. *The Palgrave handbook of international cybercrime and cyberdeviance*, 1203–1223.

88 Fegert, J. M., Vitiello, B., Plener, P. L., & Clemens, V. (2020). Challenges and burden of the Coronavirus 2019 (COVID-19) pandemic for child and adolescent mental health: a narrative review to highlight clinical and research needs in the acute phase and the long return to normality. *Child and Adolescent Psychiatry and Mental Health, 14*, 1–11.

89 See for example Chapter 5 in Halder, D. (2018). *Child sexual abuse and protection laws in India*. New Delhi: SAGE Publications. ISBN: 9789352806843.

90 Halder, D. (2017). Criminalizing revenge porn from the privacy aspects: The model revenge porn prohibitory provision. Available at https://www.livelaw.in/criminalizing-revenge-porn-privacy-aspects-model-revenge-porn-prohibitory-provision/ on 15-09-2017. Accessed on 12.12.2020.

91 Franks, M.A. (2017). Revenge porn reform: A view from the front lines. *Florida Law Review, 69*, 1251.; Citron, D.K., & Franks, M.A. (2014). Criminalizing revenge porn. *Wake Forest Law Review, 49*, 345.

92 Halder D., & Jaishankar K. (2016) Celebrities and cyber crimes: An analysis of the victimization of female film stars on the Internet. *Temida – The Journal on Victimization, Human Rights and Gender.* 19(3–4), 355–372. ISSN: 14506637.

93 Citron, D.K., & Franks, M.A. (2014). Criminalizing revenge porn. *Wake Forest Law Review, 49*, 345.

94 Kotani, J. (2017). Proceed with caution: Hate speech regulation in Japan. *Hastings Constitutional Law Quarterly 45*, 603.

95 For more detail, see Fraud and cyber crime statistics. Available at https://www.actionfraud.police.uk/fraud-stats. Accessed on 21.02.2021.

96 For more detail, see Australian Cyber Security Center (2020) *ACSC Annual Cyber Threat Report* July 2019 to June 2020. Available at https://www.cyber.gov.au/sites/default/files/2020-09/ACSC-Annual-Cyber-Threat-Report-2019-20.pdf Accessed on 21.02.2021.

97 For more detail, see Internet crime report, 2020. Available at https://www.ic3.gov/Media/PDF/AnnualReport/2020_IC3Report.pdf. Accessed on 21.02.2021.

98 For more detail, see https://ncrb.gov.in/sites/default/files/crime_in_india_table_additional_table_chapter_reports/Table%209A.9_2.pdf, and https://ncrb.gov.in/sites/default/files/crime_in_india_table_additional_table_chapter_reports/Table%209A.2_0.pdf. Accessed on 21.02.2021.

99 See Daghar, M. (2020). Wangiri targets millions of unsuspecting Kenyans. Published in https://enactafrica.org/enact-observer/wangiri-targets-millions-of-unsuspecting-kenyans on 24-11-20. Accessed on 24.12.2020.

100 Tenório, N., & Bjørn, P. (2019). Online harassment in the workplace: The role of technology in labour law disputes. *Computer Supported Cooperative Work (CSCW), 28*(3), 293–315.

101 Mumporeze, N., Han-Jin, E., & Nduhura, D. (2021). Let's spend a night together; i will increase your salary: an analysis of sextortion phenomenon in Rwandan society. *Journal of Sexual Aggression, 27*(1), 120–137.

102 Halder D., & Jaishankar, K. (2012). *Cyber crime and the victimization of women: Laws, rights, and regulations.* Hershey, PA, USA: IGI Global. ISBN: 978-1-60960-830-9.

103 Aitken, S., Gaskell, D., & Hodkinson, A. (2018). Online sexual grooming: exploratory comparison of themes arising from male offenders' communications with male victims compared to female victims. *Deviant Behavior, 39*(9), 1170–1190.

104 Ibid.

105 Halder, D., & Jaishankar, K. (2015). Irrational coping theory and positive criminology: A framework to protect victims of cyber crime. In N. Ronel, N. & D. Segev (Eds.), *Positive criminology* (pp. 276–291). Abingdon, Oxon: Routledge. ISBN: 978-0-415-74856-8.

3

VICTIMS' RIGHTS IN CYBERSPACE

3.1 Introduction

Cyber criminologists have placed users of cyberspace into three categories: States, corporations and private individuals. Often it is assumed that rights of internet users may differ with this categorisation: for example, States may claim their right to surveillance, companies may have the right to prepare their own policy guidelines for the purposes of e-commerce purposes, for regulating the grievances of subscribers, or for making their own policies for third-party liability and immunity. Similarly, an individual internet user may have the right to privacy in cyberspace, the right to free speech, and rights for restoration of justice and compensation for harm done to him/her. As may be seen from the above, the rights of each category of user may include duties or responsibilities towards the other category of the users. Similarly, rights may also include duties from fraternal users: for example, rights of a particular individual may include his or her duties not to harm the other users of cyberspace or not to unnecessarily infringe the privacy of the other. It is important to note that other than the General Data Protection Regulations prepared by the European Union parliament,[1] there are no universally binding treaties or conventions that may have codified the rights of internet users, including the victims of online harassment. This General Data Protection Regulation (GDPR) was derived from another EU convention, namely the Convention on Cybercrime, 2001, which is also known as the Budapest Convention.[2] The EU GDPR again may not be globally binding, as it is meant mainly for the EU member states. Although the EU GDPR is open to other state parties as well, several non-EU countries are now developing laws and policies on the basis of the EU GDPR.[3]

As such, rights in cyberspace may be classified broadly into two divisions: general rights of the users in cyberspace and rights of the victims of the cyber-crimes. These rights may be discussed in the context of the following basic rights: freedom of speech and expression, the right to privacy, the right to be protected against online sexual offences and the right to justice. The two categories of cyberspace rights may be interconnected. The flow chart below (Figure 3.1) explains the interconnections of these rights from the perspective of the ordinary individual's rights and the victims' rights.

The above-mentioned classification may indicate that all users (including victims and non-victims) of cyberspace may have certain rights. The term 'users of cyberspace' may necessarily include individual users and legal persons using the information and communication

DOI: 10.4324/9781315155685-3

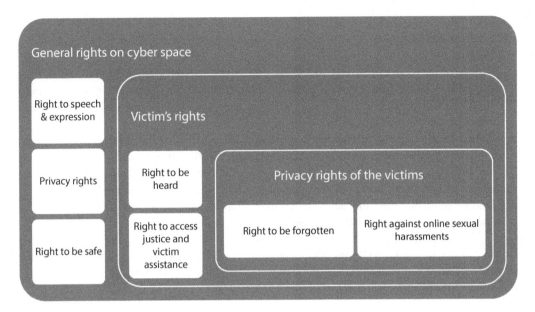

FIGURE 3.1 General rights on cyber space

technology for interacting, knowledge sharing and using cloud spaces provided by the web companies or government-supported intermediaries to store important data. 'Legal persons' may also necessarily indicate individuals operating the system on its behalf. The role of the EU GDPR, 2016 in redefining certain crucial rights of individual users is noteworthy here: the EU GDPR has placed a strong emphasis on the rights to privacy and the right to information for data breach. These rights originally flow from the Universal Declaration of Human Rights (UDHR) (1948) and the European Convention on Human Rights. The EU GDPR was brought into existence for the protection of the rights of "natural persons" in regard to the processing and free moving of personal data.[4] Article 4(1) of the Regulation further goes on to explain who can be considered as a natural person while explaining the term "personal data"; it says "an identifiable natural person is one who can be identified directly or indirectly in particularly by reference to an identifier, such as a name, an identification number, location data, an online identifier or to one more factors specific to physical, physiological, genetic, mental, economic, cultural or social identity of that natural person." This definition suggests that a natural person is a living human being who may be identified by specific physical, physiological, genetic, mental, economic, cultural or social identity that may distinguish him from any other fellow human being. The concept of natural person may be explained as "a human being who is an individual capable of assuming obligations and capable of holding rights" (Adriano, 2015).[5] The EU GDPR has limited the definition of person to this very concept of natural person. This definition in Article 4(1) therefore provides a thin line of distinction as to who may not be considered as a natural person for the purpose of this Regulation: it may not be extended to "legal person," which may have a legal personality or an artificial person (for example, government or private body or a corporate body).

Interestingly, this definition of "data subject," i.e. the "natural person" provided by the EU GDPR, may be best suited for the purpose of this book because it primarily emphasises the personal harm or victimisation that a living individual encounters online. As has been discussed in

38 Victims' rights in cyberspace

earlier chapters, it may be seen that natural persons may be subjected to different types of online victimisation and such victimisation may happen due to three main reasons:

a. Action of the States, whereby the privacy of individuals may be infringed due to state surveillance or for failure to protect the confidentiality of the data., and where freedom of speech may be censored due to suppression of the speech provisions, which are approved either by the constitution itself or by some special statutes.
b. Action of non-state actors, which may include terror organisations and corporate sectors: while the former may infringe upon the right to access the internet or the right to privacy, the latter may largely infringe upon the privacy of the users/subscribers in various ways, including data leaks, breach of confidentiality, illegal and unethical data mining, etc.
c. Interpersonal victimisation, whereby an individual may be subjected to different kinds of harassments, abuse, or victimisation by fellow human beings.

In the context of the UDHR, the EU Convention on Cybercrime and the EU GDPR, the above-mentioned rights of the users of cyberspace is discussed below with special reference to the rights of the victims.

3.2 Freedom of Speech and Expression on the Internet

Cyberspace provides a wide platform for exercising the right to speech and expression. Such speech and expression may include political opinions, scientific discoveries, the right to express one's imagination through texts and audio-visual images, etc. The internet provides a space allowing anonymity for all authors as well.[6] Cyberspace has been used for positive and negative expression of the mind. Positive expressions in cyberspace are constructive and they fall within the limits of free speech.[7] Negative expressions are destructive. These sorts of speech and expression may necessarily include hate speech, misogynist speech, and the creation, production, and distribution of illegal and non-consensual pornography materials, including revenge porn and child sexual abuse materials. Such speech is not protected by constitutional guarantees, including First Amendment guarantees in the US constitution.[8] Further, there are certain kinds of speech that may fall into grey areas, such as those that may cause harm to the recipient/target victim but are not considered illegal. Cyberbullying and trolling may be considered within this meaning. When a user or ordinary individual who may not be a user of information and digital communication technology is victimised due to the above-mentioned types of speech and expression, he/she may use his/her right to speech, which is victim-oriented. The internet may provide a wide platform for the victims of physical and online crimes to speak up and to share their concerns and frustrations and information for helping others who may have also become victims and may also be searching for information to access assistance. Once an individual has experienced any sort of victimisation, be it political, social, economic, interpersonal, etc., the concerned person typically undergoes the phase of retaliation. All victims may not avail themselves of State protection because their cases may not be recognised by the police and they may not be empowered to access justice. In cases where the victim obtains state assistance in the form of legal aid, compensation, rehabilitation, etc., he/she may take to the internet to reveal the story of victimisation and the aftereffects of the same. This may have positive as well as negative impacts. Often the victim may express opinions about the motive of the offender, the mechanisms used to execute the victimisation, how the offender may have tried to influence the criminal justice system to destroy the evidence, and how the victim may have been treated in the hands of the criminal justice machinery, including by the police before he/she received due justice. This expression/

publication may be made either by the victim him/herself on their social media profiles, blogs, YouTube or other audio-visual based internet platforms, online magazines, freely accessible academic webpages, etc., or through communicating with news channels which may have a strong online presence. A good example of this sort of speech and expression can be seen in the cases of sexual harassment of women in the workplace, whereby women victims started sharing their stories of sexual harassment with the "Me Too" hashtag. Originally starting in the United States, it has spread to many countries including Canada, Australia, South Asian countries, etc.[9] where women can freely access the internet, especially in the form of social media.[10] Further, activists and victims also took to social media and web platforms to share their views on President Trump's policies regarding travel bans to the United States directed at Muslims in 2017 and the migrant separation policy in 2018.[11] But on the other hand, the exercise of speech and expression has also resulted in a number of examples of negative expression, including that of generating fake news, which resulted in genocide (the best example could be Rohingya issue), affected international relations, and caused domestic riots in several countries.[12] Some instances where victims shared personal stories of physical space victimisation backfired on them as happened in several #MeToo cases.[13] Courts, especially in the United States, held that speech and expression restrictions such as occurred in Me Too could not be considered an infringement on the right to free speech because the person concerned had the right to express his opinion.[14] Further, victims' rights to free speech for real-life violence may extend to the right of bloggers who express their opinion about human rights violations on social media sites or blogging platforms. Although we may see this as the victim's right to express opinion and provide information, the devastating consequences that may result cannot be ignored: there were instances where bloggers from Bangladesh or Pakistan or Iraq were threatened or killed because of their blogs, which spoke out against human right violations towards specific communities (to which he/she may or may not have belonged) in physical space.[15] Reports suggested that the blogs/social media posts were read by fundamentalists and the bloggers were warned of the dire consequences for expressing their opinions before they were killed.[16] Victims of online crime may also use cyber platforms to express their anger and frustration or provide opinions and information. In such cases, retaliation may assume the form of gratifying revenge. Counter bullying is one example of such behaviour.[17] Victims may also not trust the criminal justice machinery. They may destroy evidence by deleting the offensive posts or content. Or they may not report such content to the websites for removal. They may take these measures as an expression of an irrational coping mechanism: on the one hand, they may feel extremely embarrassed and threatened for their personal safety and reputation. On the other hand, they may anticipate more harassment at the police station.[18] In such instances victims may instead take to online platforms to express their anger. This may further escalate victimisation, as the perpetrator then brings counter charges against the victim for defamation, threatening behaviour, etc.[19]

The right to speech and expression may necessarily include the right to internet access. The Universal Declaration of Human Rights provides that, every human being has the right to speech and expression and the right to access information. International civil and political rights also include the right to access information as an essential right for every human being irrespective of gender, class, race, or language. The internet has proved to be not only a platform for communication, but also an essential platform for accessing information much faster than is possible via the print media. The ever-expanding nature of the technology has made governance, education, commerce digitised. And access to the internet to take advantage of such benefits has been considered a constitutional right in many jurisdictions.[20] Right to access the internet may necessarily be seen as the right to access a digital device. It is interesting to note that there is a huge difference between developed, developing and underdeveloped countries regarding the

40 Victims' rights in cyberspace

access to digital devices. For example in the United States, Canada, Australia, and in many EU countries such as the UK, France, Germany, etc. individuals including children have access to digital devices and may actually own a digital device at a very young age. However, in countries like Bangladesh, Pakistan, Iraq, Afghanistan, Nigeria, Sudan, etc., accessing digital devices such as mobile phones and computers, including laptops, desktops, etc. may not be affordable for all.[21] In countries such as India, Saudi Arabia, Dubai, Pakistan, Bangladesh, etc., access to smart devices may be limited for women and girls, which may have a deep impact on their right to access justice, health care and education, especially when such women and girls may be victimised in the form of domestic abuse, gender discrimination-related abuse, sexual exploitation, and trafficking.[22] However, international stakeholders are working towards making access to the internet a legal right. EU courts have begun to accept the right to access the internet as a human right within the meaning of civil and political rights.[23]

But even though the right to internet access was proposed as a human right and later accepted as within the purview of human rights, this right was not considered to be equivalent to a fundamental right such as the right to speech and expression. The reason for this could be largely attributed to government censorship of web content.[24] With the huge growth of online new-sharing mechanisms, the internet began to be hit by waves of publicly accessible information, which had the potential to create civil unrest and riots, and disturb international relations among different countries, and regions. The speedy growth of the dark net and the accessibility of child sexual abuse content led a number of government agencies to restrict access to the internet for specific age group and regions.[25]

Such government restrictions have impacted the right to freedom of speech in cyberspace and the right to information from the internet. Such actions may also adversely affect victim's rights to information concerning free legal aid, emergency medical help, police webpages, etc. Indeed, the dual role of the government in exercising censorship, as well as in extending support for using e-governance, makes the right to access the internet and the right to freedom of speech and expression highly questionable.

3.3 Right to Privacy

Although the internet has provided a wide platform to access information, share information, express opinion and speech, etc., it has also caused issues of privacy infringement for ordinary individuals, including for those who may or may not use the internet. The right to privacy implies the right to be left alone. Courts have interpreted this right in various ways, including the right to bodily privacy and the right to be free from state surveillance. The right to privacy has been expanded to cover the victim's right to confidentiality, the children's right to privacy, including bodily privacy, and the accused's right to confidentiality.[26] In the internet era, the right to privacy has been interpreted as extending to digital data privacy, which has been further interpreted to include not only financial data, but also health data maintained by the health sectors, bio-metrical data—and other personal data that may be maintained by the government as well as corporate sectors—, intellectual data,[27] and other data that may be generated by the users of the internet themselves.

Right to privacy in cyberspace may be infringed upon in various ways. Research has tended to be unanimous in the view that women and children are the major victims of privacy infringement in cyberspace.[28] Such sorts of privacy infringement may include data mining for the purpose of unethical activities, including unethical gains, cyberstalking (especially in the case of interpersonal online victimisation), impersonation, creation of non-consensual pornography and revenge pornography by using mechanisms such as voyeurism, circulation of rape videos, etc.[29]

The right to privacy necessarily includes the right to protection of data by the web companies who may be collecting, processing, and storing the personal data of individuals.

A Discussion regarding liability of the companies that are data repositories and the rights of the data owners under EU GDPR is necessary here. Even though the EU GDPR created in 2016 and amended in 2018 was meant specifically for EU member countries, with the recent Facebook-Cambridge Analytica data breach case (2015) and its treatment by the EU parliament, it becomes necessary to understand the nuances of the EU GDPR.

The EU GDPR was brought into force mainly to regulate the processing of personal data in the context of the activities of the establishment of the controller or a processor, irrespective of the fact whether the processing was done within the EU territory or not. Article 3 of the EU GDPR also explains that the scope of the regulation extends to the offering of goods or services or the monitoring of the behaviour of the data subjects within the European Union. This subsection is noteworthy because it extends the scope of the Regulation to outside EU establishments as well.[30] In this context it is necessary to understand two issues of terminology that have been defined by the EU GDPR: according to Article 4(1), personal data includes any information which may best identify a natural person: this may include name, identification number, location data, any specific factor that relates to the identity of the natural person which may include mental, economic, cultural or social identity, physical physiological, genetic identity of the natural person, etc. Article 4(2) of the EU GDPR explains processing of the data which includes an operation or set of operations which is performed on personal data by manual or by automated means such as collection, recording, organisation, structure, structuring, storage, adaptation, or alteration, retrieval or consultation, use, disclosure by transmission or otherwise making it available, alignment or combination, restriction, erasure or destruction of the data.[31] Now, consider the operations that are indicated in this definition: it includes disclosure by transmission, and erasure or destruction of the data; the EU GDPR regulates such actions when these violate the privacy of the data subject; i.e. the natural persons. Article 5 further explains this by stating that such processing must be lawful, for lawful, limited and accurate purposes, and must be made in the form which permits identification of the data subject for a limited and permissible period, and it should not be retained with the controller without proper authorisation. Further, Article 5 states that such processing must be done in a secured manner. The Regulation further states that the processing would be considered lawful only for the same data subject or the natural person who may be the owner of the data, and had given lawful consent, or when there is a contractual obligation or there is a legal obligation for the processing, or when there is a legitimate interest pursued by the controller or a third party, but when such interest does not over ride any fundamental right.[32] The Regulation further clarifies that when the data is related to children, a lawful consent may be given by a child who is 16 years or older. In case the child is below the age of 16, the consent must be availed for processing of the data from natural guardian or in the absence of the same, such as a child's lawful caregiver. The Regulation further mentions that the State may provide a law to lower the age to 13 for a child to provide consent, but not below age 13. The consent (whether from adult or a child) can, however, be withdrawn for the purpose of data processing at any point of time.[33] The Regulation does prevent processing of the data which may reveal details about racial and ethnic origin, political and religious beliefs, and trade union membership; it further prohibits processing of data related to health, biometric information, sex life, sexual orientation, etc., for the purpose of unique identification of any individual person.[34] The Regulation however very clearly states that processing of the data related to criminal conviction and offences should be done in an extremely regulated manner under strict government authorisation. In relation to this, the Regulation has also laid down rules regarding the right to erasure or right to be forgotten under Article 17, whereby data subjects are given

42 Victims' rights in cyberspace

the right to reach out to the controller to erase unnecessary data, including those which are no longer relevant and that may be against fundamental rights, for which consent was not given or was withdrawn etc. The Regulation states that in such case the data must be erased without any delay.[35] The Regulation further provides certain essential rights to the data subject, including the right to transparency in regard to data processing, the right to know when personal data is collected from the data subjects, when it is not directly obtained from the data subjects, and how such data has been collected, what sort of data is collected, when it is processed, the right to restriction of the processing of the data in certain circumstances, and the right to objection, especially in cases of automated processing etc.[36]

In other words, the EU GDPR has laid down strict rules for the controller to not breach the privacy of the data subjects, and so violating their fundamental rights as well as violating the laws and rules of the EU countries. The Facebook-Cambridge Analytica data breach case (2015) is relevant here.[37] Facebook had allegedly breached the data of the data subjects to a third party, i.e. Cambridge Analytica, which initially collaborated with Facebook to conduct research on the US election. Eventually, due to the alleged negligence of Facebook, several millions of Facebook users' data (which were not relevant for the concerned research of Cambridge Analytica) got leaked to Cambridge Analytica and from there to other third parties. In the United States, some courts suggested that subscribers could launch a class petition against Facebook for such a data breach. The European Parliament summoned the Facebook CEO to show cause for such data breach, which is a punishable offence under the EU GDPR of February 2018.[38]

3.3.1 Right to be Forgotten

It may be noteworthy that all internet companies and service providers are liable to safeguard the interest of all the subscribers irrespective of their intent or motive with which they use the services. It is because of this very reason that the private information of the subscribers with which one creates an account, including the geo-location, original name, social identification number, phone numbers, and IP addresses are not revealed by the service providers and internet companies unless the subscriber him/herself reveals this information in their own profile page or messages. The liability of the internet companies and the service providers also include responding to the takedown requests for offensive comments, posts, and content that may stay on the internet for too long. The right to be forgotten is essentially connected with the right of an offender to rehabilitation and reintegration into mainstream society after he/she has undergone punishment or after he/she has been acquitted of all charges. The general criminal procedural laws suggest that the past criminal records of the offender should be kept confidential. Past criminal records of juvenile offenders should be destroyed (after securing only minimum records that may be essential for the criminal justice purposes) so that he/she is not stigmatised.[39] The internet has enabled personal information and news-related criminal offences to be available for public viewing. Internet technologies also enable viral spreading of such information. This may bring rapid fame or defamation to people whose information is so shared. In 2012, the European Parliament considered the adoption of the Right to be Forgotten on the basis of the case of two German convicted offenders who wanted Wikipedia to take down information about their criminal deeds.[40] The courts started considering such pleas for the purpose of rehabilitation of the offenders.[41] But search engine company Google posed questions about this right: Peter Fleischer of Google mentioned four types of data that may need to be considered for applying the right to be forgotten. These are (i) user-created content which the content creator may remove from the website where it has been uploaded, but which may not be removed from the search engines due to cache technology; (ii) user-created content which may be shared by third parties with/without consent of the original content creator; (iii) content about the claimant posted by others (which may include defamatory or libelous posts); (iv) content including personal identifiable information of the claimant that is stored and/or transmitted by websites.[42] Here, Fleischer indicated the victims' right to be forgotten as well. All this content may belong to the victims who want the internet to forget their 'chronicles' they uploaded, along with false information that may have been shared by a third party. Since 2012 there have been gradual developments in the right to be forgotten, especially from the perspective of website liability to take down the content as per the requests of the victims or users in general. Social media web companies over the years have created mechanisms whereby the content creators or data owners may themselves remove the contents. But in cases where such content has been virally shared in the search engines or through third parties, web companies have offered two mechanisms to remove the content: the claimants may prove their identity and demand to remove the content which they had not shared or that had been reposted by third parties without their consent. In such cases, the web companies may use artificial intelligence to detect such content that may identify the victim and may remove the content and also disable further sharing of such content. Secondly, the claimant may bring a formal court order to remove the content from the web platforms.[43] These two mechanisms strengthen the right to privacy for the victims. This mechanism also lowers the responsibility of the web companies towards content removal issues. But the success of this mechanism is still questionable: the content may be taken down from the search engines and the surface net. But the deep net may still remain inaccessible for the purpose of removing the content that the victims may feel to be unwanted and may apprehend to be violating their privacy. Further, the right to be forgotten needs to be expanded to remove the objectionable content from the personal devices of third parties, a measure which in practice may be impossible. However, we can see that the courts are adopting restriction orders in a number of interpersonal online crime-victimisation and defamation cases. This may provide some respite to the victims as the defendants may be prohibited from using the content related to the victims for further victimisation purposes.[44]

3.4 The Right to be Protected Against Online Sexual Offences

Even though the Convention on Cybercrime (2001) and its protocols mention content-related crimes such as child pornography, trafficking of children (including online child trafficking), the growth of information and digital technology has also seen the growth of online sexual slavery, especially for women and children. As has been discussed in earlier chapters, sexual offences may involve virtual slavery, including the creation of non-consensual pornography such as voyeur porn and revenge porn, sextortion, etc. It would be however wrong to presume that only women and children may be victimised by online sexual offences, including slavery. Researchers and activists have seen online sexual slavery from two different perspectives:

i online sexual slavery due to poor socio-economic conditions whereby the potential victims may have to enter into contracts for creating sexually explicit contents ether due to coercion, or they may be allured into such contracts suppressing the ultimate outcome, i.e. publishing of sexually explicit images of the persons concerned.

ii Online sexual slavery due to offline coercion, threats, etc., which may necessarily include revenge porn, non-consensual porn, etc.

Unlike the Convention on Cybercrime, 2001, there are no specific conventions or international treaties to prohibit online sexual slavery. However, the subject squarely falls under the

44 Victims' rights in cyberspace

Cybercrime convention and its protocols, which are discussed above. Further, on the basis of this very convention, several countries have developed criminal laws whereby the victims may individually or collectively bring criminal charges against the perpetrators or groups of perpetrators who may have engaged in acts of sexual slavery. Several countries have also created laws to tighten responsibility of the service providers whereby the said service providers would be liable to monitor and detect publishing of non-consensual sexually explicit images of the victims and take action against the publishers. The United States, several EU countries, and certain Asian countries, including India, Bangladesh, Sri Lanka, Malaysia, Thailand, Pakistan, Iraq, etc., have adopted stricter laws in this regard.[45] There are a few initiatives by researchers and activists from countries like the United States, India, etc., to move governments to create laws against revenge porn, which may have influenced the growth of sexual slavery particularly that resulting from interpersonal criminal activities. But such efforts have not received proper governmental support. On the other hand, international organisations including the UN Women have initiated/supported movements like #bringbackourgirls etc., which have received tremendous support and spread awareness about women and girls who may have been held captive by terror organisations and brought into sexual slavery.[46] It is pertinent to note that UN Women, UNICEF and several state-parties have now started collaborating with web companies to create better government–corporate-civil society liaisons to detect sexual slavery and take proper action.

3.5 Right to Equal Access to Justice and Fair Trial

One of the fundamental rights of victims is the right to equal access to justice and fair trial from the civil and criminal justice machinery. Cyber-crime victims are no exception. Although in cases of the government or corporate sectors being victimised, the right to equal access to justice and fair trial may be attainable because of proper execution of the laws, access to the police and courts, and the availability of cybersecurity personnel who may be able to solve the problems, in cases of individual victimisation, this becomes difficult for a number of reasons, including fear of social taboo, fear of secondary victimisation in the police station and the courts, police apathy, lack of infrastructure for investigating cyber offences, difficulty in tracing the chain of evidence, and lack of laws and policies that would force the police and the courts to acknowledge a criminal incident as an offence in cyberspace.[47] The right to equal access to justice and fair trial includes the right to legal aid, the right to a fair and public hearing in the proper forum, the right to compensation and the right to erase data in cases where such data is irrelevant and counter to the fundamental rights of the victim concerned. With the Facebook-Cambridge Analytica case, the right to equal access to justice and fair trial in cases of privacy infringement due to negligence of the service providers, has received new attention. Courts in the United States and in the European Union have started recognising the need for enforcing the payment of damages to the victims who may have suffered loss to reputation, privacy infringement, and data breach—and thereby financial loss due to negligence of the corporate entity—etc. Courts have also started emphasising the duties of the government to execute laws in a stricter manner and to set up proper monitoring and identification of any victimisation issues. However, in the majority of cases, this has remained in practice only a 'paper tiger,' since service providers/web companies have repeatedly maintained that they lack the ability to monitor each and every move of their subscribers that may have been carried out with negative aims. It is expected that more awareness about the rights of those affected by online victimisation may encourage more victims to report the crimes, which in turn may encourage the governments and courts to take stricter actions.

Notes

1 More information is available at https://gdpr-info.eu/. Accessed on 01.12.2018.
2 More information is available at http://www.europarl.europa.eu/meetdocs/2014_2019/documents/libe/dv/7_conv_budapest_/7_conv_budapest_en.pdf. Accessed on 01.12.2018.
3 For example, see the *Data Protection Act* (2018) of the United Kingdom at http://www.legislation.gov.uk/ukpga/2018/12/contents/enacted. Accessed on 01.12.2018.
4 See Chapter 1, Article 1 of the EU GDPR.
5 Adriano, E.A.Q. (2015). The natural person, legal entity or juridical person and juridical personality. *Penn State Journal of Law & International Affairs, 4*, 363. Published in http://elibrary.law.psu.edu/jlia/vol4/iss1/17. Accessed on 12.11.2018.
6 Volokh, E. (2000). Freedom of speech, cyberspace, harassment law, and the Clinton administration. *Law & Contemporary Problems, 63*, 299.
7 For a greater understanding on freedom of speech and expression in cyberspace, see Lessig, L. (1995). The zones of cyberspace. *Stanford Law Review, 48*, 1403.
8 Tsesis, A. (2001). Hate in cyberspace: Regulating hate speech on the Internet. *San Diego Law Review, 38*, 817.
9 Clark-Parsons, R. (2021). "I see you, I believe you, I stand with you":# MeToo and the performance of networked feminist visibility. *Feminist Media Studies*, 362–380; Tuerkheimer, D. (2019). Unofficial reporting in the# MeToo era. *University of Chicago Legal Forum, 21, 273.*
10 Ibid.
11 For example, see regarding Trump's migrant separation policy: Children 'in cages' in Texas. Published in https://www.bbc.com/news/world-us-canada-44518942 on 18-06-2018. Accessed on 18-06-2018.
12 For example see Al-Rawi, A. (2019). Twitter influentials and the networked publics' engagement with the Rohingya crisis in Arabic and English. In Kevin Smets, Koen Leurs, Myria Georgiou, Saskia Witteborn & Radhika Gajjala (Eds.), *The SAGE handbook of media and migration* (p. 192). UK: SAGE Publications; Marston, M. (2019). Rohingya resistance: Utilizing media to combat Buddhist-Burman nationalism. Available at https://www.nytimes.com/2018/10/15/technology/myanmar-facebook-genocide.html. Accessed on 25-12-2020
13 Tuerkheimer, D. (2019). Beyond# metoo. *New York University Law Review, 94*, 1146.
14 Ibid.
15 Bhatt, C. (2020). Words and violence: militant Islamist attacks on bloggers in Bangladesh and the United Kingdom. *Ethnic and Racial Studies*, 1–22; Khan, A.R. (2016). The political economy of digital propaganda of Islamists against liberal and secular writers and bloggers and their social movement in Bangladesh: A critical inquiry. *Religion and Social Communication, 14*, 1.
16 Ibid.
17 Halder, D., & Jaishankar, K. (2015). Irrational coping theory and positive criminology: A frame work to protect victims of cyber crime. In N. Ronel and D. Segev (Eds.), *Positive criminology* (pp. 276–291). Abingdon, Oxon: Routledge.
18 Ibid.
19 Ibid.
20 For a greater understanding of this issue, see Internet governance must ensure access for everyone – UN expert. Published in https://news.un.org/en/story/2012/05/411292-internet-governance-must-ensure-access-everyone-un-expert on 18-05-2012. Accessed on 21.12.2020.
21 Valadez, J.R., & Duran, R. (2007). Redefining the digital divide: Beyond access to computers and the internet. *The High School Journal, 90*(3), 31–44.
22 Brännström, I. (2012). Gender and digital divide 2000–2008 in two low-income economies in Sub-Saharan Africa: Kenya and Somalia in official statistics. *Government Information Quarterly, 29*(1), 60–67; Sinha, S. (2018). Gender digital divide in India: Impacting women's participation in the labour market. In Nilerd (eds) *Reflecting on India's development* (pp. 293–310). Springer, Singapore; Hobson, J. (2008). Digital whiteness, primitive blackness: Racializing the "digital divide" in film and new media. *Feminist Media Studies, 8*(2), 111–126.
23 Pollicino, O. (2019). *Right to internet access: Quid iuris? The Cambridge handbook on new human rights. Recognition, novelty, rhetoric.* Cambridge University Press. Forthcoming.
24 MacKinnon, R. (2008). Flatter world and thicker walls? Blogs, censorship and civic discourse in China. *Public Choice, 134*(1), 31–46, published by Springer.
25 Akdeniz, Y. (2001). Internet content regulation: UK government and the control of internet content. *Computer Law & Security Review, 17*(5), 303–317; Harwit, E., & Clark, D. (2001). Shaping the internet in China. Evolution of political control over network infrastructure and content. *Asian Survey, 41*(3), 377–408.
26 Byford, K.S. (1998). Privacy in cyberspace: Constructing a model of privacy for the electronic communications environment. *Rutgers Computer and Technology Law Journal, 24*, 1; Rengel, A. (2014). Privacy as

46 Victims' rights in cyberspace

an international human right and the right to obscurity in cyberspace. *Groningen Journal of International Law, 2*(2); Cohen, J. E. (1995). Right to read anonymously: A closer look at copyright management in cyberspace. *Connecticut Law Review, 28*, 981; Halder D., & Jaishankar, K. (2016). *Cyber crimes against women in India*. New Delhi: SAGE Publications. ISBN: 9789385985775.

27 Richards, N.M. (2004). Reconciling data privacy and the first amendment. *UCLA Law Review, 52*, 1149.

28 Halder D., & Jaishankar, K. (2016). *Cyber crimes against women in India*. New Delhi: SAGE Publications. ISBN: 9789385985775.

29 Ibid; Halder D., & Jaishankar, K. (2012). *Cyber crime and the victimization of women: Laws, rights, and regulations*. Hershey, PA: IGI Global. ISBN: 978-1-60960-830-9.

30 See Article 3 of the EU GDPR.

31 See Article 4(2) of the EU GDPR.

32 See for example, Articles 6 and 7 of the EU GDPR.

33 See Articles 7, 8 and 9, EU GDPR.

34 Ibid.

35 See Article 17.

36 For more information, see Articles 6 to 23 of the EU GDPR.

37 This is further explained in later chapters of this book.

38 See Hinds, J., Williams, E.J., & Joinson, A N. (2020). "It wouldn't happen to me": Privacy concerns and perspectives following the Cambridge Analytica scandal. *International Journal of Human-Computer Studies, 143*, 102498.

39 Rosen, J. (2011). The right to be forgotten. *Stanford Law Review* (Online), *64*, 88.

40 Ibid.

41 Walker, R.K. (2012). The right to be forgotten. *Hastings Law Journal, 64*, 257.

42 See for more details, Fleischer, P. (2011), Foggy thinking about the right to oblivion. *Peter Fleischer: Privacy ...?* March 9, 2011. Published in http://peterfleischer.blogspot.in/2011/03/foggy-thinking-about-right-to-oblivion.html. Accessed on 21.12.2020.

43 Halder D., & Jaishankar, K. (2016). *Cyber crimes against women in India*. New Delhi: SAGE Publications. ISBN: 9789385985775.

44 See Chapters 5 and 6 of this book for a detailed discussion of this issue.

45 This is discussed in detail in Chapter 2 of this book.

46 For a greater understanding of this issue, see Carter Olson, C. (2016). # BringBackOurGirls: Digital communities supporting real-world change and influencing mainstream media agendas. *Feminist Media Studies, 16*(5), 772–787.

47 See Chapters 5 and 6 of this book for a detailed discussion of this issue.

4

ISSUES AND CHALLENGES IN POLICING CYBER-CRIMES

4.1 Policing New Patterns of Cyber-Crimes

4.1.1 Introduction

As may be seen from the discussions in other chapters, cyber victimisation patterns have expanded. They have forced the entire policing system to take a new direction in the control of crime. With the European Union Convention on Cybercrime, 2001 (popularly known as the Budapest Convention), certain prominent patterns of cyber-crimes were recognised.[1] This convention indicated that training of the police and the criminal justice machinery needed to be more focused and, at the same time, must be more preventive and remedial in nature. State-level cyber victimisation, including attacks on confidential government data, cyberterrorism, state-sponsored cyber warfare, etc., are generally taken care of by national computer emergency response teams.[2] But in cases of cyber victimisation of companies and ordinary individuals, expert policing is needed. In the cases of companies, instances of cyber victimisation are generally tackled by hiring cybersecurity experts.[3] In this regard, mention must be made of the web companies that function as intermediaries and other companies that may be doing business in the traditional sense and who are not intermediaries. The former provide platforms for interactive discussions. They may also facilitate the company's web presence: companies may have unique profiles in platforms hosted by the web companies. Through such profiles, they may communicate with their customers/clients or potential customers, share information about their products, etc. Button (2020) has very articulately described the present arrangement by showing how web companies may engage 'content moderators' or net sweepers to remove violent content, extreme porn content, etc.[4] These content moderators may be part of outsourced agencies that support cybersecurity agencies in detecting, preventing and rectifying the damages suffered by web companies at-large, who may be offering web platforms for interaction over virtual space. These content moderators would be engaged mostly after the companies have acknowledged the reports of victimisation and have taken action to restrict its further escalation. The content moderators are generally entrusted with the duty to erase the content from the platforms so that such content may not be available in future in any platform. This helps the companies to address legal issues for takedown requests since such content may remain *floated* on the information superhighway forever, if not detected and disabled.

DOI: 10.4324/9781315155685-4

48 Challenges in policing cyber-crimes

Individual victims may however face bigger challenges in accessing help from the police for cyber-crime victimisation when compared to States and companies. States that are victimised may be able to afford remedy through its own agencies, and the issue of cross-border jurisdictions may be resolved through execution of diplomatic relations and treaties. Companies, on the other hand, may have sufficient financial resources that they may not only hire cybersecurity experts to resolve the issues, but they may also take the cases to court and hire the best lawyers available. Companies (including web companies) as defendants may also challenge the court orders for payment of huge damages, or they may also agree to pay the same. Consider the settlement of a compensation claim through a class petition in Illinois for a privacy breach by Facebook over the issue of photo face tagging of individuals. The petitioner, a privacy lawyer himself, claimed that the company had violated the privacy laws of Illinois, which provided the right to privacy against non-consensual face tagging on social media platforms. Facebook lost the case and was ordered to pay US\$650 million, which would be distributed among the victims of the said privacy breach.[5] Neither this case nor the court order would hamper the regular business of Facebook as a company. It might, however, affect the terms and policy guidelines of Facebook and their artificial intelligence system, which suggests to users to tag their friends and also themselves in photographs shared by others for better connectivity and a better online presence. Because it was a class petition and a pro bono action by the petitioner, the victims of non-consensual face tagging in Illinois could have received justice for privacy violation. But if any individual victims of such a privacy violation from any jurisdiction, including from the United States where the company is hosted, had approached the police or the court for restitution of justice as a private tort matter, he/she may not have received justice so easily.

Policing cyberspace for preventing crime victimisation targeting ordinary individuals, therefore, becomes extremely challenging because these victims may not have resources, awareness, or the physical and mental strength to endure the victimisation. These issues are discussed below:

4.1.2 New Patterns of Cyber-Crimes and Behaviour of the Victims

Since the late 1990s, patterns of cyber-crimes have rapidly changed. As discussed in Chapter 2 of this book, it can be seen that the criminality pattern has expanded from attacking computers and data to the practice of content-based crim. Again, this had expanded to targeting the privacy of the general public at large. Rapidly, the private data (which is now well connected with the governance of the State for the welfare of the general public) became a hugely profitable content area on both the surface net and the dark net. Several countries like the United States, Australia, India, the United Kingdom, etc., had deployed police officers who were originally trained to handle physical space criminal activities. Policing would be done of the basis of substantial and procedural laws addressing criminal activities. But by the beginning of the millennium, it was seen that neither the legal infrastructure, nor the police force, were able to tackle this rapid growth in cyber-crime. In some cases, police officers refused to register cases of hacking of personal computers, online frauds, or cyberstalking, as they could not believe that such kinds of offences targeting ordinary individuals occurred.[6] The presence of juveniles in cyberspace made policing even more complicated as the police officers did not know whether to apprehend the juvenile alone or whether to include the parents/guardians within the meaning of 'offenders' since it was widely believed that minors could use the internet without parental permission by means of password-protected internet connections.[7] The introduction of new platforms, their rules for privacy, and their operating methods also created challenges for policing cyberspace. Gaming apps flooded cyberspace with multiple mechanisms and game varieties. Some were specifically meant for very young children and some were meant for adolescents and adults. This widened the possibility of child-abuse, including child sexual exploitation. But the app developers were smart enough to escape the clutches of the legal enforcement authorities by showing how children have *consensually* taken part in the games with the parental identity shields.[8] Several countries have banned the functioning and operations of several web companies, including Facebook, Twitter, etc., as these companies have reportedly flouted the domestic laws regarding standards of morality.[9] But the use of proxy servers and rising criminal activities on social media platforms has created further challenges for the police in such countries.

With the introduction of the EU Convention on Cybercrime (Budapest Convention) in 2001, this perspective started changing globally. The first few years of the millennium saw a growth in research on cyber-crime patterns and researchers, practitioners, and victims started joining several academic and non-academic discussions and research projects to share their experiences and expectations concerning the police and the government at large.[10] Such discussions, research, and meetings resulted in several training manuals for police officers to tackle cyber-crimes, and State parties started creating their own laws for addressing new patterns of cyber-crimes. Several State parties like India, the United Kingdom, Philippines, Singapore, etc., created separate laws for addressing information technology-based crimes and amended their existing Penal Codes to include certain specific offences done via the internet.[11] Several other countries, including the United States, Australia, etc., amended their existing Penal Code to widen its scope to include cyber-crimes.[12] Since 2003, the UN initiated several specialised committee meetings to develop tools and modules for policing cyber-crimes, including cyber terrorism, economic fraud, child pornography, etc. These UN documents are available on the internet: most noteworthy is the United Nations Office on Drugs and Crime (UNODC) document on its Global Programme on Cybercrime.[13] State parties have since then categorised special police forces that would be trained to handle cyber-crime cases and the digital evidence to be used for trial purposes.[14]

Further, the e-governance mechanisms in most countries included a third-party presence for the maintenance of government websites and government data. These third-party stakeholders have access to the confidential private data of litigants, victims, patients, children, and employees. Even though government agencies have outsourced the responsibilities for maintenance of data to these third-party stakeholders after executing several layers of contracts between different service providers, several researchers have suggested that such contracts have been breached by the individual employees of such third parties. Research from a number of countries, including Korea, India, Bangladesh, Japan, South Africa, etc., have shown risk factors in the e-governance system.[15] It may become impossible for the police to prevent data leaking to the dark net by the perpetrators who may even have access to the performance records of the police as well. As such, the presence of the dark net has posed yet another challenge for the police administration to address cyber-crimes. The dark net was originally created in the United States for anonymous exchange of confidential military information by authorised stakeholders.[16] This is generally powered by specific software like The Onion Router Project (Tor). However, with the commercialisation of web space, the dark net has become the chosen platform for illegal weapon and drug trading. It is also the preferred platform for women and child sexual exploitation.[17] Dark net is also a chosen platform for terrorists to plan and carry out more destructive crimes. Almost all dark net-based illegal profit activities are connected with bitcoin industries. There are multiple layers of transactions of information and content in this. The buyer is connected with the seller, who may be further connected with the dark net platforms. Both the buyer and seller may be connected with the bitcoin industry, and finally, all of the above-mentioned parties in the dark net-based business are connected with the goods delivery industry, that may or may not be aware that the entire business transaction is being operated by organised gangs or that the dark net industry is involved in the business.[18] Dark net is so vigorously protected from the

50 Challenges in policing cyber-crimes

surface net that it may not be accessed by ordinary individuals—including the police—if they do not know about the secret pathways to it, i.e., the software that would enable the finder to access the dark net. In general, the police may trace out the origin of the offensive content on the online platform by searching for the IP address. The investigating officer may then obtain access to the original profile of the offender from the web platforms, which may store data about the physical address of the offender and his government-approved proof of identity. The police may also search for the digital footprints of the offenders by applying several online surveillance mechanisms. This may also include getting involved in the criminal net by using pseudo profiles, which would enable police officers to connect directly with the offender and his aides.[19] Specially-trained police officers may be able to carry out these operations once they receive the orders in question from their superiors. But this may not be the case for an ordinary victim of online monetary fraud, an advance scam, or sexual offences, who approaches the local police office for redress of his or her grievances. The investigation may not be finished as quickly as the victims may expect. This in turn may cause the victims to become frustrated with the entire criminal justice system. In the United States, high-impact cyber offences are handled by the federal police. In the civil law and common law of several countries police officers under specific police units—including national investigative agencies or dedicated cyber-crime prevention policing units—may handle such high impact cyber-crimes. The local police office may designate a police officer to initiate the investigation of any offence that may be received by such an office. Once the preliminary investigation reveals the nature and volume of the crime, the local police office may decide to hand over the case to such specialised police units. As such, a victim of online fraud or sexual offence may not always expect to be in the care of a specialised police unit even though such offences may be directly connected to the dark net.[20] Mention must be made here of certain important cases like the Giftbox Exchange case of 2016 and Child's Play case, which were interconnected cases of child trafficking that saw a joint taskforce operating from the United States and Europe. The police agency had to operate as undercover users of the platforms to access significant information for nabbing the offenders.[21] Policing the dark net may necessarily involve the rescue of victims in physical space, especially when they have been trapped by traffickers or organised criminal gangs. Policing cyber-crimes therefore needs special training and sensitisation.

Policing for regular physical space crimes requires special training to understand the nature of the case and probable impact of the crime on the victim. Training is also needed to understand the psychology of the victims: whether the victim is threatened to share the details about the perpetrator; and, if yes, why and how the victim has been threatened, etc. The police officer must also be able to understand what is the amount of damage to the property, what the relationship had been between the victim and the offender, and why the offender had taken to victimising the victim (whether it was an organised offence or whether the victim provoked the offender to commit the crime), how to collect the evidence and how to secure such evidence, how to handle the offender and the victim, how to counsel the traumatised victim, how to handle an insane, juvenile, or female offender, etc.[22] Police training also necessarily includes case management for the purpose of trial and providing protection to the victims of extreme felonies or misdemeanor cases so that the victim does not become hostile. Police officers also need to be sensitised about counselling victims so that their mental trauma may not hamper the investigative and prosecution procedures in the courts. Technical issues of policing also include monitoring crime rates in specific regions that may have reported high crime rates in the past.[23] With the passing of time, crime patterns have changed. The gender ratio of the offenders and victims in specific cases like domestic abuse, sexual violence, etc. has changed. For example, domestic violence is no more considered to be an arena where the majority of the victims would be females. Males have also starting to receive recognition as victims of domestic violence.[24] For example, researchers have called out for victim assistance for male victims of assaults in domestic violence and interpersonal victimisation cases.[25] The presence of female offenders has become more prominent in sexual offences targeting women and children.[26] This has invited more debate regarding prison management of women offenders.[27] Cases of child abuse and sexual victimisation have increasingly seen the involvement of juvenile offenders.[28] Technological developments have ushered in an era of crime victimisation where the scale of high-impact victimisation has skyrocketed: this includes environmental crimes which would harm the ecological balance, organ trafficking, terrorism—including cyberterrorism—cyber-crime victimisation, etc. These developments have tremendously impacted the existing training manuals for the police.

Cyber-crime victimisation deserves special mention here, as this type of victimisation requires special policing skills to understand the nature of the crime, measure the impact, determine the best ways to carry out the investigation, conduct the search and seizure of the digital evidence, and meet the challenges in arresting the offender. Literature shows that police officers in the 1990s were not equipped to handle a number of patterns of cyber-crimes, including hacking, cyber-stalking, adult pornography, etc., as efficiently as they would be by 2021.[29] Offences of online money laundering, job scams or lottery scams were often ignored by the police offices unless they involved a very high volume. Victims were blamed for their greed in desiring quick money and attracting predators.[30] Child pornography cases were given high priority because of the Budapest Convention and the universality of the matter. The above shortcomings of policing cyber-crimes are due to the unexpected growth of smart offenders and *unsmart* victims who would not have any knowledge about what was happening with them. Certain terrorist activities in the early millennium like the rise of the Taliban, Al Qaeda, etc., and their continuous criminal activities targeting government and private properties, hospitals, ordinary citizens, etc., kept the State parties busy in developing internal policies and laws for combatting terrorism and civil unrest that may be fuelled by terror organisations.[31] But sooner, the State parties felt the need to train and sensitise the police forces for combatting cyber-crimes due to a rising global concern for cyber-crime victimisation of men, women, and children, and, above all, due to the rising concern about this huge, illegal industry that profited from the unethical trade of personal and government data.

Policing cyber-crimes has become extremely challenging due to non-cooperation of the victims. As the nature of most organised cyber-crimes (including online economic frauds), interpersonal cyber-crimes, or victimless cyber sexual offences like sexting may suggest the involvement of victims in crime victimisation, the majority of victims often prefer not to cooperate with the police after the initial reporting of the crime victimisation, fearing victim blaming and shaming in the police station and the courts.[32] Some victims may not even provide proper evidence concerning their victimisation: they may delete the entire chat history or content or may engage private amateur hackers to remove the content before approaching the police. Some may just forward the screen shots of the message or content of the mails but without the header or any other link which thus may prevent the police officer from understanding where the crime victimisation occurred. Some victims may even suffer from withdrawal symptoms after the initial rejection of the case by the police. They may not be aware of the option of taking the matter to higher police officials or to approach the court for seeking remedy. This may allow the perpetrators (especially in cases of organised criminal gangs) to be aware of *guardian-less* victims or regions where the online criminal activities may remain unnoticed by the criminal justice machinery because of the inefficiency of the police force.[33] In many cases, victims, especially female victims, may do a complete U turn when they realise that they may not be able to cope with the influential defendants who may be able to hire the best defence lawyers available. The failure of #MeToo cases in several jurisdictions, including south Asian countries, can be attributed to this.[34] Policing such cases becomes challenging when the victim refuses to cooperate with the entire criminal justice system. The problem becomes critical with the increasing presence of bystanders. It has been observed by this author on many occasions that a victim of cyber-crime may first seek the opinion of his/her friends in determining the course of action. In this, they may share all the details that may be crucial for their own safety. Cyber bystanders may take up the content for re-sharing, assuming that it would attract huge sympathy for the victim; on some occasions, however, bystanders may also share the content for creating mashable content for their own private gain.[35] Victim management and the management of the evidence become extremely difficult for the police in such cases.

However, presently, State parties are increasingly focusing on victim-approached policing that encourages victims to participate more in the entire case management.[36] But this problem of victim cooperation remains and calls for more engagement of stakeholders.

4.2 Jurisdiction as the Biggest Challenge for Policing Cyber-Crimes

The biggest challenge for policing cyber-crimes and restitution of justice for victims is the issue of jurisdiction. In the information technology highway, the crime may be committed in one place, the defendant and victims may inhabit different places from each other and from where the crime occurred, and the effect of the victimisation may be felt in still other places. Yet, all may be connected through a common connection that may remain extremely powerful for decades. Traditional criminal law jurisprudence is generally very clear about prescriptive jurisdiction (the State's power to prescribe punishment for a wrong), adjudicative jurisdiction (the State's power of adjudicating regarding whether or not an offender has violated its prescriptive jurisdiction its jurisdiction) and jurisdiction to enforce (whereby the State may enforce and execute the laws over a defendant who has violated the laws) in cases of offline criminal activities.[37] In cases where offenders from a foreign country commits an offence within the jurisdiction of a specific country and that offence causes harm to the citizens and/or subjects of the said country, the latter may proceed to arrest the offender and try the offence as per their own laws. However, in such cases, the foreigner must be given consular access to let his/her home country know about his condition. The right to legal counselling should also not be curtailed. If, however, the offender belongs to one country, travels to another country, and commits an offence against a national of a third country, or, after committing an offence in another country against the citizen and/or property of that country, escapes to a third country or returns to his or her home country, the jurisdiction issue may become tricky. If the said offence is of a dual criminality nature, whereby the offence is recognised by the home country and the country where the offence has been committed, depending upon bilateral treaties, the offender can be extradited by one country and tried in the said country where the offence was committed.[38] Offences of a political nature, however, have been considered as exceptional cases, whereby if the person after committing the offence in his or her own country escapes to another country, the latter may not allow for extradition as may be requested by the former because there may be a threat to execute the 'offender' for sedition or rebellious acts done against the government of the former. The person may be tried as per the laws of the country where he or she has taken shelter, depending upon whether the act may at all be considered as an offence in the country where the fugitive has taken shelter.[39] This twisted tale of jurisdiction, however, is not so easy to comprehend in cyber-crime victimisation cases. There are multiple layers of jurisdictional issues in such cases. These may include the following questions:

Which country can adjudicate a case if the offender or the victim resides in the said country when the act was committed?
Is the offender extraditable in cyber victimisation cases?

Does the nature of the websites affect the decision to adjudicate and enforce the laws against the website operators?

Can a court situated in one country make the offender liable to pay compensation to the victims situated in another country?

All these questions may actually impact the powers of the police in dealing with cyber-crime victimisation cases. The Budapest Convention provides answers to the above questions:

The state parties must develop laws to recognise the offences that have been mentioned in the Budapest Convention on Cybercrime, 2001 so that no victim of cyber-crimes goes unnoticed (S.2 of the Convention on Cybercrime);

The states must develop their own system to address jurisdiction in cybercrime cases: in this regard S.3 vide Article 22 mentions the following:

1) Each Party shall adopt such legislative and other measures as may be necessary to establish jurisdiction over any offence established in accordance with Articles 2 through 11 of this Convention, when the offence is committed:

   a. in its territory; or
   b. on board a ship flying the flag of that Party; or
   c. on board an aircraft registered under the laws of that Party; or
   d. by one of its nationals, if the offence is punishable under criminal law where it was committed or if the offence is committed outside the territorial jurisdiction of any State.

2) Each Party may reserve the right not to apply or to apply only in specific cases or conditions the jurisdiction rules laid down in paragraphs 1.b through 1.d of this article or any part thereof.

3) Each Party shall adopt such measures as may be necessary to establish jurisdiction over the offences referred to in Article 24, paragraph 1, of this Convention, in cases where an alleged offender is present in its territory and it does not extradite him or her to another Party, solely on the basis of his or her nationality, after a request for extradition.[40]

© State parties shall cooperate for effective implementation of the Convention; Article 23 must be mentioned in this regard. It states as follows;

The Parties shall co-operate with each other, in accordance with the provisions of this chapter, and through the application of relevant international instruments on international co-operation in criminal matters, arrangements agreed on the basis of uniform or reciprocal legislation, and domestic laws, to the widest extent possible for the purposes of investigations or proceedings concerning criminal offences related to computer systems and data, or for the collection of evidence in electronic form of a criminal offence.[41]

In general, these questions concerning jurisdiction in cyber-crime victimisation cases are answered on the basis of two widely accepted approaches: the US approach and the European approach. The US approach speaks about Long Arm statutes, which state that local courts in the United States may obtain personal jurisdiction over the defendant under four circumstances. These are as follows:

54 Challenges in policing cyber-crimes

a. The defendant is a foreigner and has established sufficient minimum contact with the forum state, which wishes to adjudicate him/her;
b. The sufficient minimum contact with the forum state involves continuous activity by the defendant within the forum state;
c. The cause of action for prosecuting the defendant arose because of such continuous activities of the defendant within that forum state;[42]
d. The defendant would have purposefully availed himself/herself of the privilege of the illegal activities in the forum state.[43]

The European approach, on the other hand, is more inclined towards contractual obligations between the parties and the place of forum chosen by the parties. This approach is closely connected with the Brussels Regulation, 2002 on Jurisdiction, Recognition & Enforcement of Judgement in Civil & Commercial Matters[44] and the Rome Convention, 1980 on the law applicable to contractual obligations.[45] However, presently, the Sliding Scale Approach based on the nature of such websites such as passive (in case the website was a passive website and had been used just for uploading at (based on the information at the time of the commission of the offence, it may not be liable for criminal responsibilities) or interactive website (where the web company may facilitate the communication conduit and work as a channel for interaction and at the same time upload information as well), or websites of a mixed nature (where the website may be of a passive nature with very restricted interactive facilities) is also being considered for bringing the web companies within the prescriptive, adjudicating, and enforcing jurisdictions of the countries where the victims may have suffered loss/harm. To achieve this (especially to enforce domestic laws on web companies hosted in foreign locations) the courts are also relying more on the Effect Test, which is more victim-oriented than the other approaches. This test sees where the effect of the offence has been felt and how far it has impacted the victims. The Facebook Cambridge Analytica case of 2015 is the greatest example of this.[46] However, as the Budapest Convention suggests, state parties should create mutual legal assistance treaties to facilitate better policing of cyber-crimes in cases of cross-border cyber-crime issues. But except in a few cases of economic fraud, child pornography cases, espionage cases and terrorism cases, police may have to face the challenges of 'red tapisim,' which may further create frustration among the victims. Certain exceptional cases (as mentioned above) are noteworthy here, since they may show how espionage cases against state parties may have been addressed by the criminal justice machineries of different countries as a whole: Julian Assange's case is most significant here. Assange had created WikiLeaks, a whistle blower website specifically meant for exposing certain confidential government activities. In 2010 WikiLeaks allegedly leaked certain content showcasing US airstrike over Baghdad that killed several civilians. Consequently, WikiLeaks released additional confidential military documents over the following years, and Assange was charged for espionage. Being an Australian national, when he was residing in Britain, Sweden released an international arrest warrant against Assange around 2010 on charges of rape and sexual assault. Even though Assange claimed that the Swedish charges were instigated by the United States, the claim was rejected by Sweden. Assange received a bail order from the British court in this matter and he was not extradited to Sweden. But later the US authorities approached the British government for extradition of Assange for espionage against the US government. Assange sought refuge in the Ecuador embassy situated in London. He eventually was arrested in London for charges of skipping bail. But as the extradition case of the United States was taking place, even though he had finished his jail term in London, he was not freed. As per the latest reports, his extradition to the United States was not granted by the British courts.[47]

Even though the Budapest Convention pave the way towards addressing the problem of jurisdiction and several state parties have also created/amended their domestic laws to address the jurisdiction issue, many countries have not yet agreed upon the mutual legal assistance treaty, as has been mentioned in the Budapest Convention. The state parties—in order to prevent cyber-crimes, including speech crimes or hate crimes over the internet, which may disturb peace domestically and may also harm international relations—have started empowering the police force with surveillance mechanisms. Police officers authorised to carry on surveillance may use open-source intelligence and artificial intelligence to detect possible hate crimes in cyberspace. But such mechanisms have yet to be successfully used in many countries to prevent online economic offences, adult sexual offences, or interpersonal hate crimes.

Notes

1 Chapter 2 of this book has a detailed discussion on this issue.
2 Button, M. (2020). The "new" private security industry, the private policing of cyberspace and the regulatory questions. *Journal of Contemporary Criminal Justice, 36*(1), 39–55.
3 Ibid.
4 Ibid.
5 Associated Press. (2021). Judge approved $650 million settlement of privacy lawsuit against Facebook. Published in https://www.theguardian.com/technology/2021/feb/27/facebook-illinois-privacy-lawsuit-settlement on 27-02-2021. Accessed on 28.02.2021.
6 Halder D., & Jaishankar, K. (2012). *Cyber crime and the victimization of women: Laws, rights, and regulations.* Hershey, PA: IGI Global. ISBN: 978-1-60960-830-9.
7 Halder, D., & Jaishankar, K. (2016). Policing initiatives and limitations. In J. Navarro, S. Clevenger, and C.D. Marcum (Eds.), *The intersection between intimate partner abuse, technology, and cybercrime: Examining the virtual enemy* (pp. 167–186). Durham, NC: Carolina Academic Press. ISBN: 9781611636727.
8 This author had observed this in her latest research titled "PUBG as battleground between gaming app developers and government with S.69A as a poor little Queen piece" (unpublished) in the file of the author.
9 Halder D.(2017). Revenge porn against women and the applicability of therapeutic jurisprudence :a comparative analysis of regulations in India, Pakistan and Bangladesh. In D. Halder & K. Jaishankar (Eds.). *Therapeutic jurisprudence and overcoming violence against women* (pp. 282–292). Hershey, PA: IGI Global. ISBN: 978-1-60960-830-9.
10 For example, see Gercke, M. (2012). *Understanding cybercrime: Phenomena, challenges and legal response.* Available at www.itu.int/ITU-D/cyb/cybersecurity/legislation.html. Accessed on 12.12.2020.
11 Halder, D., & Jaishankar, K. (2016). Policing initiatives and limitations. In J. Navarro, S. Clevenger, and C.D. Marcum (Eds.), *The intersection between intimate partner abuse, technology, and cybercrime: Examining the virtual enemy* (pp. 167–186). Durham, NC: Carolina Academic Press. ISBN: 9781611636727.
12 Ibid.
13 Available at https://www.unodc.org/unodc/en/cybercrime/global-programme-cybercrime.html.
14 Davies, G. (2020). Shining a light on policing of the dark web: An analysis of UK investigatory powers. *The Journal of Criminal Law, 84*(5), 407–426.
15 Kudo, H. (2010). E-governance as strategy of public sector reform: Peculiarity of Japanese IT policy and its institutional origin. *Financial Accountability & Management, 26*(1), 65–84; Sarker, M.N.I., Wu, M., Liu, R., & Ma, C. (2018, August). Challenges and opportunities for information resource management for E-governance in Bangladesh. In Jiuping Xu. Fang Lee Cooke, Mitsuo Gen & Syed Ejaz Ahmed (Eds.), *International Conference on Management Science and Engineering Management* (pp. 675–688). Cham: Springer; Halder, D., & Jaishankar, K. (2020). Cyber governance and data protection in India: a critical legal analysis. In S.N. Romaniuk & M. Manjikian (Eds.), *Routledge companion to global cyber-security strategy* (pp. 337–348). E-book ISBN: 9780429399718.
16 Davies, G. (2020). Shining a light on policing of the dark web: An analysis of UK investigatory powers. *The Journal of Criminal Law, 84*(5), 407–426.
17 Ibid.
18 Ibid.
19 Ibid.
20 Mirea, M., Wang, V., & Jung, J. (2019). The not so dark side of the darknet: a qualitative study. *Security Journal, 32*(2), 102–118.

21 Davies, G. (2020). Shining a light on policing of the dark web: An analysis of UK investigatory powers. *The Journal of Criminal Law, 84*(5), 407–426.

22 Ross, J. (2011). *Policing issues: Challenges & controversies*. Burlington, MA: Jones & Bartlett Publishers.

23 Braga, A.A., Turchan, B.S., Papachristos, A.V., & Hureau, D.M. (2019). Hot spots policing and crime reduction: an update of an ongoing systematic review and meta-analysis. *Journal of Experimental Criminology, 15*(3), 289–311.

24 Letellier, P. (1994). Gay and bisexual male domestic violence victimization: Challenges to feminist theory and responses to violence. *Violence and Victims, 9*(2), 95–106.

25 Letellier, P. (1994). Gay and bisexual male domestic violence victimization: Challenges to feminist theory and responses to violence. *Violence and Victims, 9*(2), 95–106.

26 Pittaro, M. (2016). Demystifying female perpetrated sex crimes against children. *Family & Intimate Partner Violence Quarterly, 8*(4); Bloom, B., Owen, B., & Covington, S. (2004). Women offenders and the gendered effects of public policy 1. *Review of Policy Research, 21*(1), 31–48; Franklin, C.A. (2008). Women offenders, disparate treatment, and criminal justice: A theoretical, historical, and contemporary overview. *Criminal Justice Studies, 21*(4), 341–360.

27 Ibid.

28 Becker, J.V., Cunningham-Rathner, J., & Kaplan, M.S. (1986). Adolescent sexual offenders: Demographics, criminal and sexual histories, and recommendations for reducing future offenses. *Journal of Interpersonal Violence, 1*(4), 431–445.

29 Wall, D.S. (1998). Catching cybercriminals: policing the internet. *International Review of Law, Computers & Technology, 12*(2), 201–218; Wall, D.S. (2007). Policing cybercrimes: Situating the public police in networks of security within cyberspace. *Police Practice and Research, 8*(2), 183–205; Sommer, P. (2004). The future for the policing of cybercrime. *Computer Fraud & Security, 2004*(1), 8–12; Jewkes, Y., & Yar, M. (2008). Policing cyber crime: emerging trends and future challenges. In Tim Newburn (Ed.), *Handbook of policing* (pp. 580–607). Abingdon: Routledge.

30 Cross, C., & Blackshaw, D. (2015). Improving the police response to online fraud. *Policing: a journal of Policy and Practice, 9*(2), 119–128.

31 Innes, M. (2006). Policing uncertainty: Countering terror through community intelligence and democratic policing. *The Annals of the American Academy of Political and Social Science, 605*(1), 222–241; Deflem, M. (2006). Europol and the policing of international terrorism: Counter-terrorism in a global perspective. *Justice Quarterly, 23*(3), 336–359.

32 For a greater understanding of this issue, see Halder, D., & Jaishankar, K. (2011). Cyber gender harassment and secondary victimization: A comparative analysis of US, UK and India. *Victims and Offenders, 6*(4), 386–398. ISSN: 15564886.

33 Wall, D.S. (2013). Policing identity crimes. *Policing and Society, 23*(4), 437–460.

34 Tippett, E.C. (2018). The legal implications of the MeToo movement. *Minnesota Law Review, 103*, 229.

35 Holfeld, B. (2014). Perceptions and attributions of bystanders to cyber bullying. *Computers in Human Behavior, 38*, 1–7.

36 Webster, J., & Drew, J.M. (2017). Policing advance fee fraud (AFF) Experiences of fraud detectives using a victim-focused approach. *International Journal of Police Science & Management, 19*(1), 39–53.

37 Brenner, S.W., & Koops, B.J. (2004). Approaches to cybercrime jurisdiction. *Journal of High Technology Law, 4*, 1.

38 Ibid.

39 ibid.

40 See Article 22 of the Convention on Cybercrime, 2001. Available at https://www.europarl.europa.eu/meetdocs/2014_2019/documents/libe/dv/7_conv_budapest_/7_conv_budapest_en.pdf. Accessed on 02.02.2021.

41 See Article 23 of the Convention of Cybercrimes. Available at https://www.europarl.europa.eu/meetdocs/2014_2019/documents/libe/dv/7_conv_budapest_/7_conv_budapest_en.pdf. Accessed on 02.02.2021.

42 Ibid.

43 ibid.

44 See https://eur-lex.europa.eu/legal-content/EN/TXT/?uri=celex%3A32001R0044.

45 See https://eur-lex.europa.eu/legal-content/EN/ALL/?uri=celex%3A41980A0934.

46 This case is discussed in more detail in later chapters of this book.

47 Pandey, K. (2021). What is the Julian Assange WikiLeaks case? Updated on 04-01-2021 in https://www.timesnownews.com/international/article/what-is-the-julian-assange-wikileaks-case/702862. Accessed on 03.04.2021.

5

ASSISTANCE FOR CYBER-CRIME VICTIMISATION

5.1 International Instruments for Victim Assistance and Their Application for Victims of Cyber-Crimes

5.1.1 Introduction

There are no general guidelines for determining the rights of the victims of cyber-crimes except a few conventions, including the EU Convention on Cybercrime, 2001 (Budapest Convention) and the EU General Data Protection Regulations that touch upon certain kinds of cyber-crime victimisation. The right to assistance is an inherent right of victims of crimes and the abuse of power, as has been mentioned in the UN Declaration of the Basic Principles of Justice for Victims of Crime and Abuse of Power, 1985. This includes assistance in trauma recovery from the police and other frontline professionals, including doctors, lawyers, psychiatrists, and NGOs. It also includes rescue, rehabilitation, and helping the victim to return to mainstream society with dignity.[1] Cyber-crime victims may need different kinds of victim-assistance approaches due to the nature of the crime victimisation. In the majority of cases, such victims would not undergo any physical harm unless the crime victimisation fell within the category of cyber assisted offline crime, including stalking and physical assault, kidnapping, abduction, or assault on the basis of the location data, and offline property crimes, including theft or robbery on the basis of the data obtained about the victim's property and assets, and vandalising properties and assaulting victims on the basis of hate speech in cyberspace, etc. Consider the case of a Japanese pop star assaulted by her stalker who learned of her home address by analysing her location data and her facial movements captured in numerous photographs and selfies that were uploaded on social media sites[2]: after the assault, the young pop star not only needed medical assistance, but also felt extremely traumatised and unable to share anything, including information about her concerts on web platforms.[3] Again, consider the case of the victims of NHS ransomware (2017)[4]: these victims, as patients who are, had been, or would be treated by NHS stakeholders, would not get to know that their data had been taken hostage by predators unless they were to see messages or content whereby their health and sensitive personal data had been leaked. These leaks may have resulted in damage to their reputation, loss of money or threats to their security. Victims of such criminal activities may not need assistance from the police alone. They may also need the assistance of cybersecurity experts. In cases of young adults and children who may be victims of online sexual exploitation, the victim-assistance mechanism should necessarily involve rescue

DOI: 10.4324/9781315155685-5

58 Victim assistance for cyber-crime

and rehabilitation. The UN Declaration of Basic Principles of Justice for Victims of Crimes and Abuse of Power, 1985 addresses the rights of victims of crimes and abuse of power. The rights of remedy and reparation on the part of the victims of human rights have been further addressed by the Basic Principles and Guidelines on the Right to a Remedy and Reparation for Victims of Gross Violations of International Human Rights Law and Serious Violations of International Humanitarian Law, 2005, which was adopted by UN General Assembly in 2005. This chapter will discuss the rights of cyber-crime victims to remedy reparation, rescue, and rehabilitation from the perspectives of the above-mentioned two international instruments.

5.1.2 UN Declarations, Principles and Guidelines Regarding Victims' Rights

The UN Declaration of Basic Principles of Justice for Victims of Crime and Abuse of Powers (1985 Declaration) has been a landmark in the history of victimology since its formal introduction in 1947 by the French-Israeli defence lawyer Benjamin Mendelsohn.[5] This 1985 document recognised and defined the term victim and explained the difference between general crime victims and those who may be victims of abuse of power.[6] This document emphasised the need for assistance for the victims. A victim of general crimes or abuse of powers may become so vulnerable and traumatised that he/she may not be able to take any rational decision about the wellbeing of the self as well as of his/her dependants. The 1985 Declaration, therefore, addresses the responsibility of the government, NGOs, and civil society as a whole to extend help and assistance to the victims. Assistance includes the medical, material, psychological, and social assistance[7] that must be provided to the victim by the government as well as by non-government stakeholders. Victims must also be provided compensation by way of direct compensation from the offender through the criminal justice system and, where such mechanism may not be available, compensation should be made to the victim through the state fund.[8] The kinds of assistance mentioned above indicate a primary goal: restitution of justice for the victim and reintegration of the victim into mainstream society. This would be possible only when the victims are made aware of their rights and the implementation of the declaration is reflected in the national legal system of the state parties. The Declaration also highlights the need for specific training of police officers, members of the judiciary, and lawyers, especially prosecution lawyers who would be assisting the victims. This Declaration has also addressed the need for inclusion of counsellors as frontline helpers. The impact on crime-on-crime victims and victims of abuse of power may be long-lasting. This can have a detrimental effect on child survivors. The impact of victimisation may also be felt on witnesses. They may turn hostile and may even forget key points due to secondary trauma as a result of witnessing the crime victimisation. The 1985 Declaration has touched upon all these issues and has recommended every state party create a socio-legal infrastructure that will assure victims' access to justice and restitution of justice. *The Compendium of United Nations Standards and Norms in Crime Prevention and Criminal Justice* mentions capacity building, knowledge sharing, and research and training of stakeholders for the prevention of crime victimisation.[9] The concept of victim justice may not be achieved unless a proper guideline is created for the victim's right to remedy and reparation. This has been addressed in the Basic Principles and Guidelines on the Right to a Remedy and Reparation for Victims of Gross Violations of International Human Rights Law and Serious Violations of International Humanitarian Law, 2005 (2005 Guidelines). The 2005 Guidelines discussed the victim's right to remedy and reparation in cases of gross violation, international human rights, and serious violation of international humanitarian laws. Even though the terms gross violation of international human rights law and serious violation of international humanitarian laws have not been explicitly defined in the 2005 Guidelines, analysing the first paragraph of the preamble we may be able to understand the scope of these two terms. This paragraph mentions certain human rights laws found in different international documents, which are provided below:

i Article 2 of the International Covenant on Civil and Political Rights,[10] which ensures that the rights recognised by the covenant should be respected for all irrespective their race, colour, gender etc., and in case of violation of such rights, state parties should take the liability of providing proper remedy to the victim and ensure proper establishment of laws to protect such rights.

ii Article 6 of the International Convention on the Elimination of All Forms of Racial Discrimination, which speaks about protection against racial discrimination of any form and effective remedy for the same and states as follows:

States Parties shall assure to everyone within their jurisdiction effective protection and remedies, through the competent national tribunals and other State institutions, against any acts of racial discrimination which violate his human rights and fundamental freedoms contrary to this Convention, as well as the right to seek from such tribunals just and adequate reparation or satisfaction for any damage suffered as a result of such discrimination.[11]

iii Article 14 of the Convention against Torture and Other Cruel, Inhuman or Degrading Treatment or Punishment, which speaks about state party's responsibilities towards ensuring rights of the victims to redressal against unjust torture and cruel punishment, fair and adequate compensation, rehabilitation and states as follows:

1. Each State Party shall ensure in its legal system that the victim of an act of torture obtains redress and has an enforceable right to fair and adequate compensation, including the means for as full rehabilitation as possible. In the event of the death of the victim as a result of an act of torture, his dependants shall be entitled to compensation.
2. Nothing in this article shall affect any right of the victim or other persons to compensation which may exist under national law.[12]

iv Article 39 of the Convention on the Rights of the Child, which speaks about the state party's responsibilities towards ensuring physical and psychological well-being of the child victims of negligence, torture or abuse of any form and rehabilitation of the child victim and his/her and reintegration to the main stream society.[13]

   iv. Article 3 of the Hague Convention respecting the Laws and Customs of War on Land of 18 October 1907 (Convention IV), which speaks about the responsibility of the belligerent party in war to accept the liability for violating the Regulations respecting the Laws and Customs of War on Land, and pay compensation to the affected party.[14]

   v. Article 91 of the Protocol Additional to the Geneva Conventions of 12 August 1949, and relating to the Protection of Victims of International Armed Conflicts (Protocol I) of 8 June 1977, which reflects the provision mentioned in the above paragraph regarding the acceptance of the liability of the party to the conflict for violating conventions related to armed conflict and the said party's liability to pay compensation to the victims.[15]

   vi. Articles 68 of the Rome Statute of the International Criminal Court, which speaks about responsibility of the courts to protect the safety, dignity, privacy etc. of the victims and provide safer environment for the victims to participate in the criminal proceedings. It further says that all victims including victims of sexual abuse, gender abuse, child abuse etc. must be provided protection especially during the investigation and trial period. This provision also enhances its scope to cover the safety and protection of the witnesses.[16]

vii. Article 75 of the Rome Statute of the International Criminal Court, which speaks about the right to reparation of the victims and the court's responsibility to ensure adequate and just compensation to the victim either on the basis of the complaint filed by the victim or its own motion. The provision further lays down the mechanism to realise the compensation which may be paid directly by the convicted person, or it may paid from the fund created by the state party towards victim compensation.[17]

On the basis of the above international documents, the 2005 Guidelines emphasised certain principles for the realisation of justice for victims; these include a state party's obligation to respect international human rights laws and ensure respect for such laws by implementing treaties and ratifying such treaties for proper execution of the laws at the domestic level, make effective legal infrastructure to recognise and acknowledge the victims of gross and serious violation of international human rights and humanitarian laws, ensure proper investigation of the said violation of rights and take up the matter to the proper judicial forums for restitution of justice, provide equal rights to the victims to access justice and get remedy, reparation and rehabilitation for such violation of human rights, ensure protection of privacy, dignity and physical safety of the victims, create effective machinery to provide psychological care for traumatised victims and their families who may have been affected by the victimization, etc. The 2005 Guidelines placed special emphasis on just and adequate reparation to the victims to address the losses suffered by them: these include loss suffered due to physical harm, psychological trauma, financial loss generated due to the death of the only breadwinner of the family, or due to the physical and mental disability created by the crime victimisation which may have directed impacted on the continuation of the profession in which the victims was engaged, job loss, property loss, damage to reputation, etc. Clause VI of this guideline placed emphasis on treatment of the victims that should done in a humane way to not only to help him recover from the victimisation status, but also to prevent re-traumatisation. Clause IX of this guideline emphasises the issue of reparation for harm suffered by the victim/s and mentions just compensation and proper procedures to enable the victim to access the same. It also speaks about rehabilitation in the same clause with special reference to children who may have suffered gross violation of human rights.[18]

The 2005 Guidelines, along with the 1985 Declaration, have been referred to in many instances for addressing the needs of victims of racial hate crimes, discrimination,[19] armed conflicts,[20] colonial rule, and the victimisation and the long-lasting impact of the same on groups of people,[21] etc. Both these conventions have defined the term 'victim' from their own perspectives; for example, the 2005 Guidelines defined the term as follows:

> ....victims are persons who individually or collectively suffered harm, including physical or mental injury, emotional suffering, economic loss or substantial impairment of their fundamental rights, through acts or omissions that constitute gross violations of international human rights law, or serious violations of international humanitarian law. Where appropriate, and in accordance with domestic law, the term "victim" also includes the immediate family or dependants of the direct victim and persons who[22] have suffered harm in intervening to assist victims in distress or to prevent victimization.

The 1985 Declaration, on the other hand, defines the term in Clause A as follows:

1. "Victims" means persons who, individually or collectively, have suffered harm, including physical or mental injury, emotional suffering, economic loss or substantial impairment of their fundamental rights, through acts or omissions that are in violation of criminal laws operative within Member States, including those laws proscribing criminal abuse of power.

2. A person may be considered a victim, under this Declaration, regardless of whether the perpetrator is identified, apprehended, prosecuted or convicted and regardless of the familial relationship between the perpetrator and the victim. The term "victim" also includes, where appropriate, the immediate family or dependants of the direct victim and persons who have suffered harm in intervening to assist victims in distress or to prevent victimization.
3. The provisions contained herein shall be applicable to all, without distinction of any kind, such as race, colour, sex, age, language, religion, nationality, political or other opinion, cultural beliefs or practices, property, birth or family status, ethnic or social origin, and disability.[23]

Apart from the two above-mentioned international documents, there are no other specific international documents addressing cyber-crime victim's rights except the 2001 EU Convention on Cybercrime (known as the Budapest Convention).[24,25] This convention, along with the Additional Protocol to the Convention on Cybercrime, concerning the criminalisation of acts of a racist and xenophobic nature committed through computer systems, 2003,[26] Council of Europe Convention on the Prevention of Terrorism, 2005,[27] Council of Europe Convention on the Protection of Children against Sexual Exploitation and Sexual Abuse (Lanzarote Convention, 2007),[28] etc., recognised several other forms cyber-crimes, which may necessarily attract some of the characteristics of crimes, abuse of power, gross violation international human rights and serious violation of international humanitarian laws[29] that have been addressed in the 2005 Guidelines for victims' rights to remedy and reparation and the 1985 Declaration.

On the basis of this assumption, I will now discuss the rights to assistance, rescue and rehabilitation of cyber-crime victims.

5.1.3 Assistance for Cyber-Crime Victims

Unlike the victims of physical crime, abuse, and exploitation, including psychological harm, collective victimization, including exploitation from the perspective of socio-economic abuse, ethnic clashes, or terrorism, cyber-crime victims may have unique profiling (as has been discussed in Chapter 2). The government as an agency may face several cyberattacks that would harm the security infrastructure, public welfare-related data and commerce and tax-related information. Companies may suffer loss of data, economic loss, and reputation damage. Serving as the data repository of many individuals for many purposes, companies are always at risk of ransom attack and data leak. Individual users may suffer different patterns of cyberattack, varying from unauthorised access to data and devices, impersonation, online hate crimes, misogynist bullying, and sexual offences, including revenge porn, etc.

Governments and companies may have their own legal and cybersecurity expert teams to detect the problems. But this does not mean that as 'victims', they would not get the assistance within the meaning of 1985 Declaration and the 2005 Guidelines. Assistance, however, may be construed in a more sophisticated manner here: states and governments and companies may have the right to refer the matter of cyberattacks to their chosen teams of cybersecurity experts who need to maintain secrecy and confidentiality. They would not only work towards repairing the harm, but also to detect the source of the attack. In most cases of cyber warfare or espionage or unauthorised access to data, etc., governments may engage their own team of cybersecurity experts to investigate the matters with the help of the federal or national police team, who may themselves be trained in investigating computer offences. The investigation procedure generally follows the general criminal procedural practice rules, whereby the police with the help of the cybersecurity and forensic experts may need to collect the evidences and produce the entire

62 Victim assistance for cyber-crime

case details to the specified courts. In cases where the criminal justice machinery may need to conduct the investigation in foreign countries or where the fugitive offenders may reside in foreign jurisdictions, the police and the courts may seek help of the said foreign state through mutual legal agreement treaties that may exist between the said countries. The above-mentioned conventions have recognised offences related to child exploitation, including sexual abuse, economic fraud affecting interstate commerce, and terrorism, including training terrorists via the internet as offences falling within the category of universal offences,[30] whereby the state parties must cooperate with each other even if there exists no mutual legal assistance treaties. However, whether the fugitive offender may be extradited or may be tried in the country to which he/she has escaped may depend upon certain principles of jurisdictions,[31] which will be taken up later in this chapter.

Companies may seek primary assistance for cyberattacks from two stakeholders: their own team of legal and cybersecurity experts and the criminal justice machinery, including the police and the courts. Generally, cyberattacks against the companies may be of two different natures: in cases of offences targeted to the computer, data, etc., where the computer infrastructure may have been destroyed by a virus attack, Trojan attack or confidential information related to the company (not the user and/or customer data necessarily) have been stolen by cyber espionage, etc., the company may proceed to file suit for claiming compensation from the wrongdoer and this may be done through their legal team after carrying out a proper investigation, which may be done by the police. In such cases, the company may exercise its option to choose the proper forum or tribunal as per their own policies. Cases of copyright violation, trademark violation, etc., may fall under such categories. The second cases of cyber victimisation of companies may include gross infringement of data privacy. This may happen where the company works as a corporate body and as a data repository to store personal data of individuals in the categories of data related to health, banking, education, etc. Data leaking in such cases may happen for illegal profit gain. Withholding data for the purpose of ransom attack may also be a good example. In such cases, the company as a victim may obtain assistance from the criminal justice machinery directly. The impact of such kinds of victimisation may be so great that many thousands of people are affected. The case of the NHS ransomware attack is a good example: the hospital as a corporate body may be considered as a victim as well as a liable party for the data breach. As a liable stakeholder, such corporate bodies may be sued by individuals whose data has been affected. But in such instances companies or organisations generally prefer to take the stand as a 'victim' so that their cases may be handled by the federal police or competent national investigating agencies. Doing so also lowers their responsibility towards the primary data owners who may seek compensation from such companies or organisations for their negligence in providing secured infrastructure for securing their data. It must be remembered here that companies and organisations cannot themselves go ahead and investigate the matter or they would breach the rights of other legal personalities. Instead, they have to avail themselves of the services of the police for collection of evidence, tracking the perpetrator/s, making arrests, producing the case dockets to the courts, and assisting the prosecution for conducting the trial.

The issue of victim assistance, rescue, and rehabilitation in cases of cyber-crime victimisation becomes more significant from the perspective of individual victims, who may lack the access to customised cybersecurity or legal experts that governments and companies have. Moreover, they may not be able to cope with the financial loss, reputation damage, psychological harm, threats—including threats to physical integrity—as easily as companies or governments. Reasons for this include lack of awareness, lack of resources to support oneself in such kinds of victimisation and the chances for re-victimisation due to their vulnerability (especially when the victims are minors, senior citizens, people belonging to socio-economically disadvantaged

Victim assistance for cyber-crime **63**

classes, or women). Victim assistance in this case can be discussed under three headings: (i) NGO/voluntary-based assistance, (ii) intermediary-based assistance and (iii) criminal justice machinery-based assistance.

5.2 Victim Assistance from Non-Governmental Stakeholders

The 1985 Declaration includes non-government organisations (NGOs) for extending assistance for the victims of crime by stating as follows in clause 14:

> Victims should receive the necessary material, medical, psychological and social assistance through governmental, voluntary, community-based and indigenous means.[32]

However, such organisations must be trained to understand the nature of the specific cases of criminal offence, what may be the impact of such offence on the victims who may have suffered the harm and how the impact of victimisation and traumatisation may be minimised.[33] NGOs or voluntary organisations, however, are not the police. Nor are they the courts. They cannot take the law in their hands and cannot proceed to investigate the matter as the police may do. In cases of crime victimisation, the scope of such organisations becomes limited to helping the victim become connected with the police and courts and provide help to the victim to reduce the trauma: for example, in cases of trafficking, they may offer to help the victim in rehabilitation, reintegration with mainstream society and assistance in accessing compensation from the courts.[34] But under no circumstances can they interrogate the victims or confine the accused on the basis of preliminary information that may be available from the victim or from circumstantial evidence. To do so could lead to further crime victimisation for the victim as well as the accused, as the principles of justice and fair trial would not be met in such cases. NGOs may also work with funds received from sponsors and funders for different purposes: these may include awareness building, research, including empirical research for publishing literature in specific crime victimisation cases, building infrastructure for rescue and rehabilitation of the victims, etc.[35] But the mission of the NGOs should not be influenced by any political manifesto because this might adversely affect the overall mission of assisting crime victims. Similarly, NGOs must also not exploit the private and confidential information of the victims for their own research and publication interests unless these are shared consensually by the victim/s.[36]

Presently, there are several NGOs/voluntary organisations working towards assisting cyber-crime victims all over the world. For example, consider the workings of Working to Halt Online Abuse (WHOA),[37] Centre for Cyber Victim Counselling (CCVC),[38] or the Cyber Civil Rights Initiative,[39] Cybersafety.org,[40] etc. These organisations, located in different parts of the world, work towards counselling victims of cyber-crimes sharing information and awareness about different kinds of cyber-crimes, different legislations addressing cyber-crimes in different regions, etc. Some of the founders and board members have also proposed preventive laws against revenge porn,[41] cyberstalking,[42] etc. The NGOs may also coordinate with international stakeholders in creating policy guidelines for safer digital environments for people at large.[43] These NGOs/civil society organisations should also be considered for coordination by tech companies like Google, Facebook, etc., for imparting information regarding the latest developments in their own policies and terms so that such NGOs may in turn coordinate with the general public, educational institutes, and childcare institutes to create awareness about safe digital environments. The social workers and founders of such organisations may also be invited by the government offices to train the police, prosecutors, and magistrates to understand the nature of the crimes, handle the digital evidence, and help the victims in receiving remedy

64 Victim assistance for cyber-crime

when the latter approaches the criminal justice machinery for restitution of justice. However, it has also been observed that there are several individuals and civil society organisations who may offer help in lieu of money to the victims of cyber-crimes: these offers may include promises to remove the offensive and defamatory contents from social media platforms and to pierce the privacy veils to expose the identity of the accused, etc. Such kinds of offers cannot be supported if seen from a legal perspective. Victims of card frauds, impersonation, revenge porn, defamation, etc., may not be willing to wait for the lengthy legal procedures which may include filing police reports, carrying out investigations, search and seizure of the digital evidences, preparing the case files for prosecution and trial, etc. Victims may need quick redress of grievances, especially in cases where they may feel that they may have taken active part in their own victimisation: this need may be explained from the perspective of the Victim Precipitation Theory,[44] which suggests that victims may initiate their own victimisation by making a relationship with the perpetrator/s and leading them to cause the victimization, due the former's ignorance and the latter's successful efforts at manipulation. Consider the cases of online fraud; in cases of lottery scams, advance scams, or job scams, the greed of the victim for quick gain may push him or her to accept the offer of the perpetrator, ultimately leading to the former's loss.[45] Again, in cases of online sexual offences or cyberstalking where the victims are not completely innocent but may feel that they have been victimised due their own online lifestyle that may have exposed their profiles to the predators,[46] they may fear shame and blame. In order to hide their embarrassment and at the same time, carry out a remedial measure, they may seek quick removal of the contents and may connect with hackers.[47] NGOs and civil society organisations and individuals, who may be experts in cybersecurity and who wish to offer help to the victims of cyber-crimes, should restrain themselves from offering such kinds of promises and executing victim redress in such irrational ways. On the contrary, NGOs and civil society organisations should counsel the victims for preventing future harm and contact the police and web companies for restitution of justice in a legal manner. It must be noted that criminal procedural laws may permit individuals who are not police officers to restrain an accused of any felony or any indictable offence, etc. to prevent him or her from escaping, or engage in collecting evidence, and safekeeping the same for the purpose of cooperating with the police and hand over the accused and the evidences unharmed.[48] Applying the same principle, it may be understood that if the NGO or the civil society member comes across any information of cyber-crime victimisation and the victim approaches them with accurate information (especially in cases of interpersonal cyber-crimes including cyberstalking, voyeurism, revenge porn, or phishing scams where the victim may share the name/email id/phone number etc., of the accused), the said NGO or the civil society member or the civil society organisation must provide the police with the digital footprints that they may have accessed.

5.3 Victim Assistance from Intermediaries

Every web company working as an intermediary or service provider to enable people to share information, network, and access information on the worldwide web through information and digital communication technology has certain responsibilities towards the users and non-users who may be affected by such information and knowledge sharing through their platforms.[49] These responsibilities include removal of offensive contents reported by the users/victims and cooperation with the criminal justice machinery in providing information about the offender/s who may have violated the laws by misusing the web platforms for illegal activities, including illegal profit gain by online economic fraud, unauthorised access to data/device and illegal modification of the same, malicious virus attacks, ransom attacks, teaching and recruiting for cyber terrorism, cyber victimisation of children, including online sexual exploitation, and interpersonal cybercriminal activities, including cyberstalking, cyber sexual offences, etc. These responsibilities fall within the meaning of due diligence for the intermediaries which ensures that the intermediaries have not knowingly hosted any content that may be offensive or violated laws, including infringement of copyrights, etc., have not generated these contents knowingly, do not earn profits from such content, and have developed mechanism to receive complaints from the victims. These responsibilities protect the intermediaries from third-party liability, especially for removal of contents on a Good Samaritan basis, which flows from S.230© of the Communication Decency Act and in regards to immunity from copyright infringement-related matters, flowing from S.512 of the Digital Millennium Copyright Act (DMCA).[50] Every intermediary—including those offering interactive web platforms like e-commerce platforms, social media companies, messaging platforms, or passive web platforms which may be used only for sharing certain information—now have customer/user care sections where they may receive requests for reporting copyright infringements, content removal, content blocking and flagging of the said content/s so that the same content may be prevented from being further shared in the same platform or in the search engines, etc. The said section is also responsible for responding to the victims/aggrieved parties with their decision regarding the reported contents. The websites (especially the e-commerce platforms) also bear the responsibility in accepting grievances from users/customers related to the product quality, service/product delivery by the original seller/ service providers.[51] Generally, all web companies/intermediaries may need to take action on grievance reports within the shortest possible time, which may vary according to the domestic laws of different countries. But the intermediaries/web companies cannot be disinterested in the matter of the reports. In cases where the reported contents fall within the categories of offensive contents as per the rules and policies of the intermediaries/web companies, they must assume responsibility not only to remove the content from their own platform, but also to block the sharing of the content by perpetrator/s through anonymous profiles and multiple platforms by applying artificial intelligence mechanisms.[52] The intermediaries, however, have self-imposed restrictions for sharing user data with anyone other than the police and courts. Hence, they would not be liable to share the information about the original identity, location, and IP address of the perpetrators with the victims. But they must share the such information with the police and courts if the victim prefers to lodge complaints with the criminal justice machinery. While the intermediaries/web companies must create mechanisms to accept takedown/content violation reports and share information about their terms and policies which must mandatorily showcase information about safer digital environments for adults and children, removal of any content which may not fall within the meaning of online child abuse, including child sexual abuse, cyberterrorism, racial hatred, etc., may largely depend on the domestic laws of the website where it is hosted. It is for this very reason that several web companies hosted in the United States may reject the content removal request if it is related to bullying, hate comments, trolling, or adult pornographic contents. The First Amendment guarantees of the US constitution have been considered as a main challenge in this regard.[53] But in such cases, the victims may reach out to the police and courts to obtain an order for taking down the contents and revealing the identity of the perpetrator. The web companies must mandatorily cooperate in such cases. If they however deny or fail to cooperate with the courts, the web companies/intermediaries may face penal sanctions from the criminal laws of the countries where the victim have felt the effect of victimisation.[54]

However, with the strict implementation of EU General Data Protection Regulations, the failure of web companies to secure the privacy of users/subscribers is illustrated in a numbers of cases: the biggest example might be the Facebook Cambridge Analytica case where the data of

66 Victim assistance for cyber-crime

several million Facebook users was shared non-consensually with Cambridge Analytica (2015), a company that was researching the US election and Donald Trump's campaign for presidential candidature.[55] The questioning of Facebook CEO Mark Zuckerberg by the European Parliament in 2018 in the matter of Cambridge Analytica and the sharing of fake news has been considered a historic event in the chorology of the development of internet regulatory laws and Facebook was subsequently sued for their negligence to control the data breach of millions of people.[56]

5.4 Victim Assistance from the Criminal Justice Machinery

A victim of online fraud, harassment, or sexual offences may necessarily access the criminal justice machinery for restitution of justice. This is a fundamental right of every victim. But the procedure for victim assistance for restitution of justice may not be the same for online crimes as for traditional criminal activities, including in causing bodily harm or damage to property or in cases of offline ethnic clashes, domestic violence, or child abuse cases. In contemporary times police officers around the world are trained to handle cyber-crime offences. In most countries there are special police teams to handle issues related to co-identity and integrity of government data, online economic offences, cyber espionage, online child sexual abuses, deep dark net-related offences, etc. The police power to investigate certain offences, however, may be limited due to the void in the legal infrastructure that exists in specific countries: for example, in many countries revenge porn is not recognised as an offence;[57] some countries may not engage in treaties with others to exchange fugitives in cases of cyber-crime, or even for mutual legal assistance for the investigation of cyber-crime cases, etc.[58] But in most cases of cyber-crime victimisation (as has been discussed in Chapter 2 of this book), the police and courts must offer their assistance for restitution of justice. In cases where companies may become victims of cyber-crimes due to data theft, copyright infringement, cyber espionage, broad scale Trojan attack, or ransom attack, their representative/s may approach the police for filing criminal cases. There have been numerous cases of sabotage of companies in recent years as well. Consider the case of Anthony Levandowsky who was charged for theft of Google's trade secrets related to research on autonomous vehicles. The federal prosecutors pressed for a huge bail bond and putting Levandowsky under surveillance to restrict his freedom of movement.[59] And consider the case of the American electric car manufacturing company Tesla that had sued several employees for alleged breach of trade secret, data theft and damage to the business and to the reputation of the company in the market.[60] In all such cases, companies may engage their own investigators in fact-finding and may then report the matter to the police for bringing a formal criminal case against the perpetrator. In certain cases where the business organisation is a small startup company, it may completely rely on the police for procedural aspects of the investigation, searches, making arrests, etc., and taking the matter to the prosecutor directly. In all cases where companies present as victims, the general trend of seeking remedy is in seeking damages from the defendants. The prosecutors may press the courts to award jail sentences for the defendant as standard punishment for the offences. Most companies working as data repositories tend to prefer launching suits for data breaches because they do not wish to themselves be targeted by law suits from the original data owners whose data may have been breached while in custody of the companies. In contrast to the Facebook Cambridge Analytica case, the NHS cyberattack case (2017) (where hospital data of several millions of people were affected) could be a good example in this regard. The former was alleged to be a matter of gross negligence on behalf of the company: in the latter case, the NHS as an organization—along with several other companies and government organisations—was considered as a victim of a cyber ransom attack. The US justice department had reportedly traced the culprit behind the wide scale ransom attack (whose scope was not limited to the NHS ransom attack in the United Kingdom). The Department of Justice charged Park Jin Hyok for this ransom attack, an individual who was alleged to have connections with North Korea.[61]

In cases of individual victimization, including interpersonal online victimisation, the police may initiate investigation after considering the nature of the crime. In both common law and civil law countries, offences such as online economic fraud, child online sexual abuse, and grooming of individuals—including young adults and adolescents—for the purpose of cyberterrorism are dealt with by federal police or officers from national investigation agency teams. This is because such crimes may have international connections and the impact of the said crimes may have a deeper and graver impact on the national economy and internal peace and security. Most countries in the world have categorised such offences as felonies or indictable offences or cognisable offences where the police may start investigation without the order of the magistrate.[62] But when it comes to interpersonal crimes, there may be several challenges for police action: for example, in bullying and trolling cases, the police may not consider the case as a serious offence unless the victim feels threatened for life or for bodily injury, or the victim had already suffered physical/bodily injury, or it falls in the category of racial abuse.[63] However, in certain cases police may treat such online bullying and trolling incidents as serious offences if the text of the message falls within the meaning of indecent speech or targeting communal harmony of the region. A good example could be the case of a British woman who was arrested for allegedly sending offensive text over the WhatsApp to her former flatmate in Dubai.[64] Considering the strict laws related to indecent speech in Dubai, police action in this case was indeed exceptional when compared with similar incidents found in the United States or United Kingdom. As such, responses vary from country to country as restrictive speech laws are not uniform. Again, police action on reports of uploading impersonating profiles or still images to mislead people regarding the identity and reputation of the victim may vary in different regions. Presently, in most countries, if a complainant lodges a complaint regarding uploading of content that is impersonating in nature, the police may apply local laws to categorise this as a serious offence or misdemeanor, especially when the intention of the defendant may be to have illegal gain or harm the reputation of the victim. Even though there may be several challenges for policing cyber victimization—discussed in the next chapter—police may offer restitution of justice to the victim in a legal way, far preferable to irrational strategies that may be taken up by victims themselves for quick removal of contents. The police may use their special power to communicate with the websites to access information about the offender.[65] This may also enable the police to take the matter formally to the courts to press for charges so that the offender is punished and the victim obtains due justice, including compensation.

It must also be understood that the courts may be the ultimate authorities for deciding the quantum of punishment for the offenders and damages/compensations for the victims. Even though many victims may not wish to take their cases to the police, fearing further secondary traumatisation in the police station, prosecutor's office, or courts, the latter may apply its judicial discretion to offer the best remedial measures to the victim/s; consider the Canadian case of *Caplan v. Atas* (2021).[66] The court acknowledged a *'new common law tort of internet harassment'*[67] as a remedial mechanism to prevent internet harassment through bullying, stalking, publishing defamatory content, etc. of employees at the workplace and ordered a permanent injunction to the defendant from harassing the plaintiffs and their families and other victims of the former's defamatory and harassing posts. The court also permitted the plaintiff to take action with the help of the legal machinery for removal of the offensive contents on the ground that such posts were false and defamatory.[68] The criminal justice machinery may also take steps for rescuing and rehabilitating victims of online crimes, especially when it relates to young victims, particularly adolescents who may be victimised by online sexual exploitation, including child sexual

68 Victim assistance for cyber-crime

exploitation. The Philippine case of the rescue of 13 women (2020) is noteworthy here: on reliable information, the government authorities, including the police, searched specific locations in Butuan in the Philippines and rescued 13 women and children who had been forced to act in sexual shows on the internet on the basis of the customised demands of the clients. These victims were later handed over to a women and child protection centre, and the suspected offenders were arrested by the police on the basis of the regional anti-trafficking act (Anti-Trafficking in Persons Act of 2003 [Republic Acts of the Philippines] R.A. No. 9208), anti-child pornography act (Anti-Child Pornography Act of 2009, R.A. No. 10175), cyber-crime prevention act (Cybercrime Prevention Act of 2012), etc. existing in the Philippines.[69]

These examples may show that the government criminal justice machinery may provide better victim assistance than the amateur individual hackers or ethical hacking companies often chosen by the victims as mechanisms to cope with the victimisation.[70] However, the criminal justice machinery may not provide adequate assistance for the victims unless the civil society organisations and web companies jointly support it for successful investigation, prosecution, and delivery of a sentence. Restitution may also include removal of offensive content from all web platforms, permanently banning the defendant from using the information of the victims for creating further damaging contents, and rescue and rehabilitation of the victims, if necessary. It is only when the three above-mentioned stakeholders jointly create awareness about victim justice and victim assistance in a rational and legal way that we will see more victims trusting the criminal justice machinery and participating in the justice delivery process.

Notes

1 This is discussed at length in the next segment of this chapter.
2 See Stalker 'found Japanese singer through reflection in her eyes'. October 10, 2019. Published in https://www.bbc.com/news/world-asia-50000234 on 10-10-2019. Accessed on 10.10.2019.
3 Ibid.
4 See NHS 'could have prevented' WannaCry ransomware attack. Published in https://www.bbc.com/news/technology-41753022 on 27-10-2017. Accessed on 12.12.2019.
5 Wemmers, J.A. (2010). A short history of victimology. *Victimology, victim assistance and criminal justice: Perspectives shared by international experts at the inter-university centre of Dubrovnik.*
6 Refer to Chapter 1 for a discussion about victims.
7 For a greater understanding of this issue, see Compendium of United Nations standards and norms in crime prevention and criminal justice. Available at https://www.unodc.org/pdf/compendium/compendium_2006_part_03_02.pdf. Accessed on 01.02.2021.
8 Ibid.
9 Ibid.
10 Article 2 of the International Covenant on Civil and Political Rights mentioned as below:

1. Each State Party to the present Covenant undertakes to respect and to ensure to all individuals within its territory and subject to its jurisdiction the rights recognized in the present Covenant, without distinction of any kind, such as race, colour, sex, language, religion, political or other opinion, national or social origin, property, birth or other status.
2. Where not already provided for by existing legislative or other measures, each State Party to the present Covenant undertakes to take the necessary steps, in accordance with its constitutional processes and with the provisions of the present Covenant, to adopt such laws or other measures as may be necessary to give effect to the rights recognized in the present Covenant.
3. Each State Party to the present Covenant undertakes:

   a. To ensure that any person whose rights or freedoms as herein recognized are violated shall have an effective remedy, notwithstanding that the violation has been committed by persons acting in an official capacity;
   b. To ensure that any person claiming such a remedy shall have his right thereto determined by competent judicial, administrative or legislative authorities, or by any other competent

authority provided for by the legal system of the State, and to develop the possibilities of judicial remedy;

c. To ensure that the competent authorities shall enforce such remedies when granted.

11 See https://www.ohchr.org/en/professionalinterest/pages/cerd.aspx. Accessed on 20.01.2021.

12 See https://www.ohchr.org/en/professionalinterest/pages/cat.aspx#:~:text=Article%2014&text=Each%20State%20Party%20shall%20ensure%20in%20its%20legal%20system%20that,as%20full%20rehabilitation%20as%20possible. Accessed on 20.01.2021.

13 Article 39 of the Convention of the Rights of the Child states as follows: States parties shall take all appropriate measures to promote physical and psychological recovery and social reintegration of a child victim of: any form of neglect, exploitation, or abuse; torture or any other form of cruel, inhuman or degrading treatment or punishment; or armed conflicts. Such recovery and reintegration shall take place in an environment which fosters the health, self-respect and dignity of the child.

14 For a greater understanding of this issue, see Article 3 of the Laws and Customs of War on Land (Hague, IV). Available at https://www.loc.gov/law/help/us-treaties/bevans/m-ust000001-0631.pdf. Accessed on 20.01.2021.

15 See Article 91 of the Protocol Additional to the Geneva Conventions of 12 August 1949, and relating to the Protection of Victims of International Armed Conflicts (Protocol I) of 8 June 1977. Available at https://www.un.org/en/genocideprevention/documents/atrocity-crimes/Doc.34_AP-I-EN.pdf. Accessed on 20.01.2021.

16 Article 68 of the Rome Statute of the International Criminal Court states as follows: Protection of the victims and witnesses and their participation in the proceedings

1. The Court shall take appropriate measures to protect the safety, physical and psychological well-being, dignity and privacy of victims and witnesses. In so doing, the Court shall have regard to all relevant factors, including age, gender as defined in article 7, paragraph 3, and health, and the nature of the crime, in particular, but not limited to, where the crime involves sexual or gender violence or violence against children. The Prosecutor shall take such measures particularly during the investigation and prosecution of such crimes. These measures shall not be prejudicial to or inconsistent with the rights of the accused and a fair and impartial trial.

2. As an exception to the principle of public hearings provided for in article 67, the Chambers of the Court may, to protect victims and witnesses or an accused, conduct any part of the proceedings in camera or allow the presentation of evidence by electronic or other special means. In particular, such measures shall be implemented in the case of a victim of sexual violence or a child who is a victim or a witness, unless otherwise ordered by the Court, having regard to all the circumstances, particularly the views of the victim or witness.

3. Where the personal interests of the victims are affected, the Court shall permit their views and concerns to be presented and considered at stages of the proceedings determined to be appropriate by the Court and in a manner which is not prejudicial to or inconsistent with the rights of the accused and a fair and impartial trial. Such views and concerns may be presented by the legal representatives of the victims where the Court considers it appropriate, in accordance with the Rules of Procedure and Evidence.

4. The Victims and Witnesses Unit may advise the Prosecutor and the Court on appropriate protective measures, security arrangements, counselling and assistance as referred to in article 43, paragraph 6

5. Where the disclosure of evidence or information pursuant to this Statute may lead to the grave endangerment of the security of a witness or his or her family, the Prosecutor may, for the purposes of any proceedings conducted prior to the commencement of the trial, withhold such evidence or information and instead submit a summary thereof. Such measures shall be exercised in a manner which is not prejudicial to or inconsistent with the rights of the accused and a fair and impartial trial.

6. A State may make an application for necessary measures to be taken in respect of the protection of its servants or agents and the protection of confidential or sensitive information.

17 Article 75 of the Rome Statute of the International Criminal Court states as follows: Reparations to victims

1. The Court shall establish principles relating to reparations to, or in respect of, victims, including restitution, compensation and rehabilitation. On this basis, in its decision the

Court may, either upon request or on its own motion in exceptional circumstances, determine the scope and extent of any damage, loss and injury to, or in respect of, victims and will state the principles on which it is acting.

2. The Court may make an order directly against a convicted person specifying appropriate reparations to, or in respect of, victims, including restitution, compensation and rehabilitation. Where appropriate, the Court may order that the award for reparations be made through the Trust Fund provided for in article 79.

3. Before making an order under this article, the Court may invite and shall take account of representations from or on behalf of the convicted person, victims, other interested persons or interested States.

4. In exercising its power under this article, the Court may, after a person is convicted of a crime within the jurisdiction of the Court, determine whether, in order to give effect to an order which it may make under this article, it is necessary to seek measures under article 93, paragraph 1.

5. A State Party shall give effect to a decision under this article as if the provisions of article 109 were applicable to this article.

6. Nothing in this article shall be interpreted as prejudicing the rights of victims under national or international law

18 See the Basic Principles and Guidelines on the Right to a Remedy and Reparation for Victims of Gross Violations of International Human Rights Law and Serious Violations of International Humanitarian Law. Available at https://www.ohchr.org/en/professionalinterest/pages/remedyandreparation.aspx. Accessed on 20.01.2021.

19 Desmet, E. (2008). The UN Basic Principles and Guidelines on the Right to a Remedy and Reparation: A landmark or window-dressing? An analysis with special attention to the situation of indigenous peoples. *South African Journal on Human Rights, 24*(1), 71–103.

20 Droege, C. (2007). The interplay between international humanitarian law and international human rights law in situations of armed conflict. *Israel Law Review, 40*, 310.

21 Van Boven, T. (2013). Victim-oriented perspectives: Rights and realities. In Thorsten Bonacker & Christoph Safferling (Eds.), *Victims of international crimes: an interdisciplinary discourse* (pp. 17–27). The Hague, The Netherlands: TMC Asser Press.

22 See Clause V of the Basic Principles and Guidelines on the Right to a Remedy and Reparation for Victims of Gross Violations of International Human Rights Law and Serious Violations of International Humanitarian Law.

23 See the Declaration of Basic Principles of Justice for Victims of Crime and Abuse of Power. 1985. Available at https://www.ohchr.org/en/professionalinterest/pages/victimsofcrimeandabuseofpower.aspx. Accessed on 20.01.2021.

24 For a greater understanding of this issue, see https://rm.coe.int/1680081561. Accessed on 22.01.2021.

25 These Conventions have been discussed in detail in Chapter 2 of this book which looks at patterns of cyber-crime victimsiation.

26 See for more information https://www.coe.int/en/web/conventions/full-list/-/conventions/treaty/189. Accessed on 20.01.2021.

27 See for more information https://www.coe.int/en/web/conventions/full-list/-/conventions/treaty/196. Accessed on 21.01.2021.

28 See for more information https://www.coe.int/en/web/conventions/full-list/-/conventions/treaty/201. Accessed on 21.01.2021.

29 Chapter 2 of this book provides a greater discussion of this issue.

30 Moore, S. (2013). Cyber attacks and the beginnings of an international cyber treaty. *North Carolina Journal of International Law and Commercial Regulation, 39*, 223.

31 Ibid.

32 See https://www.unodc.org/pdf/compendium/compendium_2006_part_03_02.pdf. Accessed on 12.02.2021.

33 Ibid.

34 Villacampa, C., & Torres, N. (2019). Human trafficking for criminal exploitation: Effects suffered by victims in their passage through the criminal justice system. *International Review of Victimology, 25*(1), 3–18.

35 Petras, J. (1999). NGOs: In the service of imperialism. *Journal of Contemporary Asia, 29*(4), 429–440.

36 Ibid.

37 See NGO at https://www.haltabuse.org/about/about.shtml.

38 See NGO at https://www.cybervictims.org/.

39 See https://www.cybercivilrights.org/welcome/.

40 See https://www.cybersafety.org/.

41 For example, Dr. Mary Anne Franks of the Cyber Civil Rights Initiative had proposed a statute to combat revenge porn in the United States. (More about this can be found at https://www.cybercivilrights.org/ccri-board/. The organisation provides a list of States that have revenge porn laws. Available at https://www.cybercivilrights.org/revenge-porn-laws/. In India, this author was the first to propose a revenge porn law, and the published draft proposal can be found in Halder, D. (2017). *Criminalizing revenge porn from the privacy aspects: The model revenge porn prohibitory provision*. Available at https://www.livelaw.in/criminalizing-revenge-porn-privacy-aspects-model-revenge-porn-prohibitory-provision/.

42 Jayne Hitchcock, founder of Working to Halt Online Abuse, had proposed a cyberstalking law in the United States. For more detail, see http://www.jahitchcock.com/cyberstalked/.

43 Consider General Comment No. 25 (2021) on children's rights in relation to the digital environment, which in Clause V explicitly mentions the responsibility of the State parties to identify the civil society organizations working for safe digital environments for children and coordinating with such organizations towards policy making etc. The General comment is available at https://www.ohchr.org/EN/HRBodies/CRC/Pages/GCChildrensRightsRelationDigitalEnvironment.aspx. Accessed on 24.03.2021.

44 Miethe, T.D. (1985). The myth or reality of victim involvement in crime: A review and comment on victim-precipitation research. *Sociological Focus*, 209–220.

45 Cross, C. (2013). 'Nobody's holding a gun to your head …': Examining current discourses surrounding victims of online fraud. In Crime, Justice and Social Democracy: Proceedings of the 2nd International Conference, 2013, Volume 1 (pp. 25–32). Crime and Justice Research Centre, Queensland University of Technology.

46 Leukfeldt, E.R., & Yar, M. (2016). Applying routine activity theory to cybercrime: A theoretical and empirical analysis. *Deviant Behavior, 37*(3), 263–280.

47 Halder, D., & Jaishankar, K. (2015). Irrational coping theory and positive criminology: A framework to protect victims of cyber crime. In N. Ronel, N. & D. Segev (Eds.), *Positive criminology* (pp. 276–291). Abingdon, Oxon: Routledge.

48 For example, S.24A of the *Police and Criminal Evidence Act*, 1984 (PACE Act) allows any other person other than a police officer to arrest a person accused of indictable offence. But this does not mean that the former may harm or injure or detain the latter without proper legal authorities.

49 Such non-users may be victims whose data, including images, may have been accessed /captured without their knowledge and consent for illegal profit gain. For example, consider the case of Jarawa tribal women who were illegally photographed in Andaman in 2012 as part of alleged 'human safari' on the Andaman island of India (See Halder D., & Jaishankar, K. (2014). Online victimization of Andaman Jarawa tribal women: An analysis of the 'human safari' YouTube videos (2012) and its effects. *British Journal of Criminology, 54*(4), 673–688. ISSN: 00070955)

50 Edwards, L. (2012). Role and responsibility of internet intermediaries in the field of copyright and related rights. (April 21, 2012). Available at http://www.wipo.int/copyright/en/doc/role_and_responsibility_of_the_internet_intermediaries_final.pdf.150. Accessed on 12.02.2021.

51 Consider the 'contact us' page for Google at https://about.google/contact-google/?hl=en_GB. Another example is the security and privacy page of Amazon.com which guides users towards terms and policies of the website and helps users understand the reporting mechanism. Available at https://www.amazon.in/gp/help/customer/display.html?nodeId=GLSBYFE9MGKKQXXM. Similarly, see Facebook's page at https://www.facebook.com/help/1753719584844061/?helpref=hc_global_nav for policies and reporting violations of rights.

52 Holt, T.J. (2018). Regulating cybercrime through law enforcement and industry mechanisms. *The ANNALS of the American Academy of Political and Social Science, 679*(1), 140–157.

53 Citron, D.K., & Norton, H. (2011). Intermediaries and hate speech: Fostering digital citizenship for our information age. *Boston University Law Review, 91*, 1435. Halder, D., & Jaishankar, K. (2016). *Cyber crimes against women in India*. New Delhi: SAGE Publications. ISBN: 9789385985775.

54 Brenner, S.W., & Koops, B.J. (2004). Approaches to cybercrime jurisdiction. *Journal of High Technology Law, 4*, 1.

55 Kozlowska, I. (2018). *Facebook and data privacy in the age of Cambridge Analytica*. Seattle, WA: The University of Washington. Available at https://heinonline.org/HOL/LandingPage?handle=hein.journals/jhtl4&div=3&id=&page=. Accessed on 02.12.2020. Retrieved August, 1, 2019.

56 Criddle, C. (2020). Facebook sued over Cambridge Analytica data scandal. Published in https://www.bbc.com/news/technology-54722362 on 28-10-2020. Accessed on 21.12.2020.

57 Halder D. (2017). Revenge porn against women and the applicability of therapeutic jurisprudence : A comparative analysis of regulations in India, Pakistan and Bangladesh. In. D. Halder & K. Jaishankar (Eds.). *Therapeutic jurisprudence and overcoming violence against women* (pp. 282–292). Hershey, PA: IGI Global. ISBN: 978-1-60960-830-9.

72 Victim assistance for cyber-crime

58 This is discussed in Chapter 6 of this book.

59 Isaac, M. (2019). Former star google and uber engineer charged with theft of trade secrets. Published in https://www.nytimes.com/2019/08/27/technology/google-trade-secrets-levandowski.html on 27-08-2019. Accessed on 12.01.2021.

60 Kolodney, L. (2021). Tesla sues former employee for allegedly stealing software code. Published in https://www.cnbc.com/2021/01/22/tesla-sues-former-employee-for-allegedly-stealing-software-code.html on 22-01-2021. Accessed on 22-01-2021.

61 See Busby, M. (2018). North Korean hacker charged over cyber attacks against NHS. Published in *The Guardian*. https://www.theguardian.com/world/2018/sep/06/us-doj-north-korea-sony-hackers-chares on 06.09.2018. Accessed on 21.01.2021.

62 Holt, T.J., Cale, J., Leclerc, B., & Drew, J. (2020). Assessing the challenges affecting the investigative methods to combat online child exploitation material offenses. *Aggression and Violent Behavior, 55*, 101464. Available at https://prohic.nl/wp-content/uploads/2020/11/2020-11-19-ChildExploitationMaterialInternetIn-vestigation.December2020.pdf. Accessed on 12.01.2021; Cross, C. (2020). 'Oh we can't actually do anything about that': The problematic nature of jurisdiction for online fraud victims. *Criminology & Criminal Justice, 20*(3), 358–375. Cross, C. (2018). Expectations vs reality: Responding to online fraud across the fraud justice network. *International Journal of Law, Crime and Justice, 55*, 1–12.

63 Halder D., & Jaishankar, K. (2012). *Cyber crime and the victimization of women: Laws, rights, and regulations*. Hershey, PA: IGI Global. ISBN: 978-1-60960-830-9.

64 See GulteDesk (2021) UK woman jailed in Dubai for 'F word' on WhatsApp. Published in https://www.gulte.com/trends/57487/uk-woman-jailed-in-dubai-for-f-word-on-whatsapp on 06-02-2021. Accessed on 06.02.2021.

65 The principles of due diligence make it mandatory for all web companies to cooperate with the police and the courts. See for more detail on this issue Oliva, J R., Morgan, R., & Compton, M.T. (2010). A practical overview of de-escalation skills in law enforcement: Helping individuals in crisis while reducing police liability and injury. *Journal of Police Crisis Negotiations, 10*(1–2), 15–29.

66 *Caplan v. Atas*, 2021 ONSC 670. See https://www.canlii.org/en/on/onsc/doc/2021/2021onsc670/2021onsc670.html?autocompleteStr=Caplan%20v.%20Atas%2C%202021%20ONSC%20670&autocompletePos=2. Accessed on 01.03.2021.

67 Ibid.

68 Ibid.

69 See Fermin, M. (2020). Baby, 12 others rescued from cybersex den in Butuan. Published in https://philippineslifestyle.com/baby-12-others-rescued-from-cybersex-den-in-butuan/ on May 22, 2020. Accessed on 21.01.2021.

70 16. Halder, D., & Jaishankar, K. (2015). Irrational coping theory and positive criminology: A frame work to protect victims of cyber crime. In N. Ronel and D. Segev (Eds.), *Positive criminology* (pp. 276–291). Abingdon, Oxon: Routledge. ISBN 978-0-415-74856-8.

6

PENOLOGY FOR CYBER VICTIMISATION

Criminal Justice and Societal Responses

6.1 The Ever-Expanding Dimension of Penology

Often, penology for general crime victimisation is discussed in light of five major theories, namely, the deterrent theory of punishment, which suggests that punishment should aim at creating fear in the minds of ordinary people that would stop them from committing a similar crime, the preventive theory of punishment which aims at preventing the commission of the offence and eliminating the criminal mindset in offenders by preventing them from committing offences and/or repeating the offences, the retributive theory of punishment which aims to make the offenders suffer in the same manner as they made their victims suffer, and the reformative theory of punishment which aims to reform the offender through a systematic correctional administration system so that the offender may be rehabilitated and reintegrated into the mainstream society.[1] The theory and practice of penology took a new direction with the work of Enrico Ferri, who emphasised the involvement of victims in the penological framework by way of their right to compensation.[2] Cyber-crime victimisation differs from general (offline) crime victimisation due to the issue of anonymity, the possibility of the involvement of multiple stakeholders from different jurisdictions, the lack of focused laws to deal with emerging issues of cyber victimisation, the poor infrastructure in the criminal justice machinery to deal with online victimisations, etc. This chapter will analyse the scope of existing theories for understanding the penology of cyber victimisation in light of existing legal practices of prescribing punishment for different types of victimisations, including unauthorised access and modification of content, cyberterrorism, phishing, cyberstalking, online bullying, non-consensual and revenge porn, online child pornography, etc.

Victimology cannot be viewed without penology, just as criminology may not be understood outside of the context of penology. Victims' rights necessarily include the right to be compensated and the right to have the wrong repaired and wound healed. Seen from the perspective of modern victimology, it is the duty of the State to accommodate victims in the penological settings of the criminal justice mechanisms. Penology in general deals with the science of punishment. It deals with that branch of criminal justice science that views punishment as a preventive, punitive, or rehabilitative mechanism to prevent the further escalation of crimes. The existing literature on penology suggests that penology is a study of inflicting proper quantum of punishment on the offender.[3] The earlier application of modern penology was primarily associated

DOI: 10.4324/9781315155685-6

74 Penology for cyber victimisation

with the administration of punishment: slowly, with the growth of restorative and rehabilitative punishment theories, studies of penology have expanded their scope to encompass correctional administration.[4] The subject of penology is deeply connected with the criminal law and criminal justice administration. A legal understanding of punishment for interpersonal crimes and violent crimes—including sexual abuse crimes—terrorism, economic crimes, property crimes, etc., have undergone a sea change since the 1940s.[5] In many jurisdictions for instance, capital punishment has been abolished as a penalty for violent crimes. Correctional administration has replaced the punishment of death, solitary confinement, and custodial torture as mechanisms for administering punishment for crimes, including violent crimes. In correctional administration, a further emphasis has been placed upon rehabilitation and reintegration of the offender into mainstream society. In this setup, victims' needs have sometimes been overshadowed by the rights of the accused for rehabilitation and reintegration. Unlike the ancient or the 'golden period of victimology,' when victims would have the right to decide the form of punishment for the offenders, modern victimological and penological understanding shifts the responsibility of punishing the offender to the State. Punishment has to be awarded as per the quantum of the crime and States cannot inflict punishments as per the wishes of the victims. The quantum of punishment has to be decided in a very systematic way where the rights of the offender are also considered. Victims may necessarily be compensated and/or rehabilitated in this setup. In cases of violent crime, offences targeting properties and misdemeanor cases, the modern criminal justice administration indicates that victims may be benefited by preventive detention of the offender and also by way of victim compensation that would be paid by the State and/ or by the offender directly in certain cases.[6] Modern penological ideologies have been tremendously affected by the principles of restorative justice and the reformative theory of punishment. According Zehr and Gohar (2003), in terms of restorative justice, "justice begins with a concern for victims and their needs; it seeks to repair the harm as much as possible, both concretely and symbolically. This victim-oriented approach requires that justice be concerned about victims' needs even when no offender has been identified or apprehended."[7] The reformative theory of punishment, on the other hand, speaks about reformation of the accused through the correctional punitive system. This has been well articulated by D.J.B Hawkins (1944). According to him, reformation "is really procured through punishment, when the delinquent realises that he has deserved his punishment and ought to amend himself."[8]

In the latter half of the 1970s, Justice Krishna Iyer of the Supreme Court of India introduced the concept of Therapeutic Jurisprudence specifically for the offenders. He was greatly influenced by the sociological school of jurisprudence and the realistic movement of jurisprudence in the United States.[9] He observed the conditions of Indian prisons that were bearing the imprint of the colonial past: prisoners convicted with a death sentence or life imprisonment or long-term jail sentences were treated inhumanly in many south Asian countries until the 1970s. Anger and frustration pushed the offenders to an even more negative mental state. Iyer suggested that unless the prisons became therapeutic in practice, offenders would never be able to improve.[10] Much later, the concept of therapeutic jurisprudence was formally developed for the wellbeing of the offenders as well as of the victims by Bruce Winnick and David Wexler in the 1980s.[11] Therapeutic jurisprudence combines several approaches for considering the type and quantum of punishment: it mixes restorative justice, reformative approaches, and compensatory jurisprudential approaches, along with the wellbeing of victims and offenders. The law here is used as a therapeutic and healing tool, just as medicine is used as a healing tool for patients.[12] Courts across the United States started experimenting with therapeutic jurisprudence, especially for mental health-related cases, drugs and narcotics addiction- related cases, and in cases regarding sexual offenders, juvenile offenders, and domestic violence.[13] However, except in academic discussions, therapeutic jurisprudence has not yet been considered for victim justice in cyber-crime cases.[14]

6.2 Critical Analysis of Punishments Prescribed by Different Jurisdictions for Cyber Offences

Online victimisation by way of interpersonal crimes, including stalking, bullying, doxing, impersonation, unauthorised access to devices and data, creation and distribution of non-consensual and revenge porn materials, etc.; or by way of financial crimes, including phishing, job scams, lottery scams, etc.; or crimes against the State and corporations,. including cyber espionage, cyber warfare, cyberterrorism, ransom attacks, data tampering, inflicting malicious viruses, etc. may need to be addressed differently from a penological perspective. It must be noted that the earliest forms of cyber-crimes included attacks against the government data, especially that of the military intelligentsia, and corporate data.[15] This pattern of offence still exists in all jurisdictions, and stakeholders have expressed concern that such sorts of attacks are becoming more organised. In such cases S. 1030 18 US Code (fraud and related activity in connection with computers) may be traditionally applied in the United States, which prescribes punishment of pecuniary fines and jail terms that may go up to 20 years. The provision also allows for the confiscation of property that may have been used for committing the offence. It explains in the first paragraph why such unauthorised access may be considered as a heinous crime: such offences include intentional access to the confidential information of the government which cannot otherwise be accessed by public. It involves the knowledge on the part of the offender that such information and the devices which are used to store the information, cannot be and should not be accessed by anyone unless there is an executive order for such action. This provision further mentions that to merit punishment under this provision, the information needs to be connected to national defence and the military intelligentsia, interstate trade, diplomatic relationships with other countries and/or important data which is connected to the public administration and welfare of the nation. This provision further mentions that in order to qualify as an offence under this section, the prosecution must establish that the offender had accessed such information and had communicated or tried to communicate or transmitted or tried to transmit the said information to others also not authorised to receive such information. The provision mentions that the offence also includes retaining the information unauthorisedly, which the offender may use for any illegal purposes, including asking for money to release such information.[16]

This provision provides punishment both in the form of fines and jail terms. As has been stated above, the maximum amount of jail sentence for unauthorised access to confidential information, and illegally transmitting/conveying the said information or retaining the same is up to 20 years, and this is applicable for an offender who may have already undergone a jail term for some other offence. In short, the quantum of the punishment may increase in cases where the offender repeats his or her offensive behaviour of violating the laws.[17] The quantum of punishment is reduced in cases of illegally and unauthorisedly accessing the said information with a purpose of commercial gain or private financial gain. But this sentence may be doubled if the offender is found to be a habitual offender.[18] This provision indicates that sentencing may differ on the basis of three aspects: (i) when the effect of such damaging of confidentiality affects the internal security and administration system to an extent where enemy states and non-state actors may find the situation extremely vulnerable, (ii) when such acts causes bodily injury in the physical space of others, and (iii) when the damage may be repaired and the effect of the damage may be controlled. It may also be seen that the US system in this regard also considers the behaviour of the offender and the effect of his or her previous conviction. It considers the issue of the offender's past criminal experience. The State may be an extremely vulnerable victim to offenders who are aware of the cost of the confidential military and government information and the how to obtain unauthorised access to protected computers. The above-mentioned provision, therefore, also emphasises use of preventive restriction mechanisms for offenders.

Section 2701 of Chapter 121, USC 18 (Part 1) which is applied as preventive legislation, may also be considered here. This legislation makes it an offence to (a) intentionally accesses without authorisation a facility through which an electronic communication service is provided, or in other words attacks the computer and computer networks as a whole and disrupts the right to use the electronic communications; or (b) intentionally exceed authorisation to access that facility, or in other words 'hacks and cracks' in other's data without the owner's permission; However, it is interesting to note how the language of the second paragraph of this provision suggests punishment depending upon the motive of the accused; when the 'offence' is done with a motive to gain for "commercial purposes, malicious destruction or damage, or private commercial gain, or in furtherance of any criminal or tortuous act in violation of the Constitution or laws of the United States or any State," which may very well justify cases of hacking and cracking confidential information of companies or ordinary individuals, including accessing the private information of women and children, morphing victim's pictures and accessing and sharing information for the online commercial adult entertainment industry, or even the defamation and humiliation of the victim before an internet audience, etc. The law provides monetary fines and imprisonment sentences ranging from 5 to 10 years. In other cases, when such activities are not done for the purposes as stated above, but done for mischievous reasons like making fun of the victim, harassment, etc., the law provides punishment with fines and imprisonments which may range from 1 to 5 years, depending on whether the offence is a first offence or has been committed after a conviction.[19]

In the United Kingdom, on the other hand, unauthorised access to computers, computer data, etc., are dealt with by the *Computer Misuse Act* (1990). Three types of offences are recognised under this provision, which includes unauthorised access to computer material, enabling other parties for such unauthorised access, and unauthorised modification of the confidential content. The penalties may include summary conviction. But if such acts lead to grave offences against the nation, the punishment may be heavier. In all such cases where a defendant is proved to have committed spying and has passed the confidential information to enemy stakeholders, then he or she would be liable for punishment as shall be the case for felony under the *Official Secrets Act*, 1911."[20] In almost all jurisdictions, cyber espionage has been considered the heaviest offence for which the defendant may be prescribed punishment for felony. Harbouring spying, however, may be considered as a misdemeanor.[21] If the offence of unauthorised access to protected information leads to the commission of cyberterrorism, and which in turn may lead to massive destruction of lives and properties in real life, State parties may be authorised to prescribe the heaviest punishment, including capital punishment. The example of the US air strike over Al Qaeda supremo Bin Laden may be pertinent here: the 9/11 Twin Tower attack was closely related to unauthorised access and hacktivism of civil aviation computers.[22] It resulted in widespread destruction of human lives and properties. Even though the US government had indicted Bin Laden with charges of terrorism, he was not available for prosecution purposes. He was later alleged to have been killed in the May 2012 US airstrike in Abbottabad, Pakistan where he was allegedly hiding. The US government was heavily criticised for such kinds of 'assassination'.[23] In 2008, India witnessed another terrorist attack, which included terror outfits gathering information from social media posts. Lashkar-e-Taliba carried out this terror attack on 26 November, 2008 in which armed terrorists stormed Taj Hotel in Mumbai, which at the time was hosting international guests and a few diplomatic meetings. Some terrorists of the same group targeted a Jewish synagogue and killed several inmates. Two had reached the railway station and had carried out mass killings. During the incident, members of the terror group were continuously receiving suggestions of routes for their next destination, and means to escape the police and army barricades by members from different jurisdictions who were updating them on the basis of social media posts by ordinary individuals.[24] Most of the terrorists were killed by the army when they tried to escape. One survived, and he was arrested and tried by the courts in India for charges of terrorism. He was even provided a defence lawyer by the free legal service authorities of the court in order to exercise his right to a fair trial. The trial court sentenced him with capital punishment and the Supreme Court of India confirmed the sentence. He was executed in 2012, as per the court order.[25] However, some of the aides of the 26/11 terror groups were arrested in the United States for aiding them in thewir terror activities and are undergoing long prison sentences in the United States.[26,27] Clearly, in the case of cyberterrorism resulting in death and/or destruction in the physical world, the practice has been to use the deterrent theory of punishment but with a coating of retributive theory. If it does not result in physical space destructions and deaths, States generally adhere to deterrent and preventive theories of punishment. In cases of unauthorised access for financial gain, states may generally rely on the preventive theory of punishment with deterrence as the baseline. The aim of punishment in such cases is two-fold: to prevent offender from having access to confidential information and to prevent them from committing any further damage to the entire system which may help them access the information later. Long-term imprisonment may or may not guarantee reformation for the offenders because the offenders may, with their knowledge of hacking and cracking, repeat the offences. These offenders, therefore, may not be allowed to interact with other offenders who may be serving lesser sentences and who may be influenced by the former to continue working in their vicious network. States may take this opportunity to improve the cybersecurity infrastructure. Simultaneously, States may also fine the offender/s. This pecuniary 'gain' may be added to state funds for victim justice. States and/or companies may, however, create bad examples by engaging such offenders for ethical hacking. This practice may not create any deterrence in the society, especially for young offenders since they may know that such offences may fetch rewards for them from the 'victim'.

However, a different outcome may result in cases of cyber espionage or data theft for companies. Companies face financial losses for such sorts of offences. Hence, in such cases the punishment may be of a hefty civil penalty. The victim may proceed with civil suits for damages and civil imprisonment. Tesla's case may be a good example in this regard.[28] Similarly, copyright and trademark-related offences may also fall within the category of civil offences. But in the case of the quantum of loss being greater and the consequences leading to fraudulent activities targeting general individuals, the case may be considered as a serious misdemeanor. Such cases may occur due to the greed of the offender. In all such cases, the aim of the punishment can be focused towards reformative justice. When it comes to victimisation of individuals by way interpersonal crime victimisation, the situation may be different. Crime-victimisations may here be divided into two groups as follows (see Figure 6.1).

FIGURE 6.1 Major types of cyber-crime victimisation

78 Penology for cyber victimisation

As may be seen in the above, the first category includes bullying, trolling, hate speech, misogynist speech, defamation, etc. In most jurisdictions, including the United States, the United Kingdom, Canada, Australia, India, Singapore, etc. cyberbullying and trolling may not be considered serious offences unless they instigates self-harm or cause physical assault, discrimination and hate crimes to the victim in real life.[29] These may be treated as problem behavioural patterns when offenders are adolescents. Where, however, the offence may cause severe mental trauma to the victim and there are statutory prohibitory orders available for the offence, the offender may be retrained from posting any further communication to the victim and pay fines and/or compensation to the victim.[30] Here, the ultimate aim of the punishment is preventive so that harm does not escalate. In certain cases, the court may also consider suggesting payment of fine by parents so that the parents may execute their responsibility for the wrongs committed by their children. In cases of online defamation that may happen through trolling or by sharing defamatory statements with a third party, the cases may be considered misdemeanors and the defendants may need to accept their charges in the pretrial hearing itself. The penological understanding in such cases could be quite similar to that in domestic abuse cases where the courts may decide to impose restrictions on the perpetrator-partner in contacting the victim. If the defendant fails to maintain the restriction orders, he may be charged with serious misdemeanors, which may depend on the impact of the offensive behaviour on the victim. In cases of grave instances of defamation, where the perpetrators may make the defamatory statement 'viral' by sharing on multiple platforms, courts may order the perpetrator to take on the burden of removing the contents. Such offences may be categorised as misdemeanors.[31] Here, two aspects must be seen for the purpose of sentencing: (a) mens rea, which is reflected in the sadistic pleasure of the perpetrator when the defamatory contents are not only uploaded, but also virally spread on cyber platforms. The perpetrator wants millions of people to read and see the false stories and the humiliation of the victim/s. (b) actus rea: whereby the perpetrator may choose such platforms which may attract more 'readers'. The perpetrator may know that even if the victim complains about one or two pieces of content available on one or web pages, the same content may still be available on multiple platforms and may surface one by one. He or she may engage other readers/users/viewers to share the post/content for further humiliation of the victim. Citron (2014) suggested that civil society members should help the victim recover from such defamation by posting more positive contents about the victim. It should be a community effort. This measure was driven by the reasoning and good conscience of people who wanted to support the victim because the courts would not know how to deal with multiple pages of online defamation and at whose cost. But the recent Canadian case of *Caplan v Atas* (2021)[32] has not only made the courts acknowledge a new tort of internet harassment, but has also brought in a new era of cyber penology. The court in this case could understand that if the perpetrator is ordered to remove the content from the platforms, he/she would be given a way out to commit the same offence again with the same excuse for escaping the clutches of the law. Rather, the court decided to impose a restraining order from publishing anything about the victim.[33] Here, we can see a trend for punishment especially for bullying, trolling and defamation cases (not amounting to causing physical harm and instigation to self-harm). The courts would rather take the preventive approach coupled with a reformative approach to the punishment. A remedial approach for victim justice may include an order to pay compensation for reputation damage. But in certain cases the perpetrator may make the plea of being bankrupt as happened in the above-mentioned Canadian case. In such cases, the victims may have to rely upon monetary relief provided by the state relief fund. This may completely depend upon the discretion of the court and the financial and emotional impact of the speech offence on the victim. Remedial measures may also be executed through third-party actions, whereby the courts may ask the police and/or the websites to remove the defamatory contents. Here, the websites may also become liable for contempt of their court order and they may also be liable to be charged for violating due diligence if they fail to remove the content after the same had been ordered by the court.

Speech crimes (as discussed above) and offences for privacy violation may share one thing in common; i.e., threat to harm, which attracts a heavier punishment than does a summary conviction. There is again a difference between a threat to harm and an actual harm suffered by the victims. Cases of cyberstalking, grooming for data mining, receiving communications which are 'designed' for monetary fraud, etc., may fall into the category offences where the punishment should not only be focused towards prevention of speech and privacy violations, but also the consideration of the threat created by the perpetrator to commit harm. This is reflected in certain laws on cyberstalking: consider the anti-cyberstalking law in the United Kingdom. In the United Kingdom, the primary law for cyberstalking is the *Protection from Harassment Act*, 1997, which prescribes a summary conviction of imprisonment for 51 weeks or a fine, or both.[34,35]

The United States also offers a federal cyberstalking law under US Code 18 Section 2261A, which states:

Whoever (1) travels in interstate or foreign commerce or within the special maritime and territorial jurisdiction of the United States, or enters or leaves Indian country, with the intent to kill, injure, harass, or place under surveillance with intent to kill, injure, harass, or intimidate another person, and in the course of, or as a result of, such travel places that person in reasonable fear of the death of, or serious bodily injury to, or causes substantial emotional distress to that person, a member of the immediate family (as defined in Section 115) of that person, or the spouse or intimate partner of that person; or (2) with the intent (A) to kill, injure, harass, or place under surveillance with intent to kill, injure, harass, or intimidate, or cause substantial emotional distress to a person in another State or tribal jurisdiction or within the special maritime and territorial jurisdiction of the United States; or (B) to place a person in another State or tribal jurisdiction, or within the special maritime and territorial jurisdiction of the United States, in reasonable fear of the death of, or serious bodily injury to (i) that person; (ii) a member of the immediate family (as defined in Section 115 [1] of that person; or (iii) a spouse or intimate partner of that person; uses the mail, any interactive computer service, or any facility of interstate or foreign commerce to engage in a course of conduct that causes substantial emotional distress to that person or places that person in reasonable fear of the death of, or serious bodily injury to, any of the persons described in clauses (i) through (iii) of subparagraph (B); [2] shall be punished as provided in Section 2261 (b) of this title.

The penalties mentioned in the above paragraph includes the following:

A person who violates this section or section 2261A shall be fined under this title, imprisoned–(1) for life or any term of years, if death of the victim results; (2) for not more than 20 years if permanent disfigurement or life threatening bodily injury to the victim results; (3) for not more than 10 years, if serious bodily injury to the victim results or if the offender uses a dangerous weapon during the offense; (4) as provided for the applicable conduct under chapter 109A if the offense would constitute an offense under chapter 109A (without regard to whether the offense was committed in the special maritime and territorial jurisdiction of the United States or in a Federal prison); and 5) for not more than 5 years, in any other case, or both fined and imprisoned.[36]

80 Penology for cyber victimisation

It must also be noted that the United States offers no contact order, temporary or permanent civil or criminal injunction and restraining order, as mentioned in Ss.6 of S.2261 of US Code 18. Similarly, the UK legislation also offers civil as well as criminal remedies, which include restriction and no contact orders and also summary convictions. But in India the legislation offers different remedies. Cyberstalking is regulated by S.354D of the Indian Penal Code which considers stalking, including cyberstalking, as a behavioural offence.[37] As may be seen, S.354D of the Indian Penal Code is essentially a women-centric law."[38]

The penological approach in such cases is towards restraining the defendant from executing further harm. In certain cases, the court may also order a protection order to the victim for a short duration which may be reciprocated with the 'no contact order' against the defendant. But obtaining such orders is still considered a huge task for many victims, as the act of cyberstalking may not be considered a grave offence in many jurisdictions unless the harm has already been created.[39] Cases of grooming for purposes of economic fraud also do not receive heavy punishments in most jurisdictions. They may result in summary convictions when the prosecution may prove that the perpetrator was impersonating someone for fraudulent purposes. The focus of punishment shifts to the commission of identity theft and/or impersonation for the purpose of commission of economic offences and/or sexual offences. S. 18 U.S. Code § 1028 which speaks about "Fraud and related activity in connection with identification documents, authentication features, and information" states that punishment for such impersonation may lead to a minimum 15 years of jail term and/or fine.[40] Other jurisdictions also offer similar heavier punishments for impersonation for committing economic frauds and/or sexual offences.

Feeling threatened depends upon several other factors: has the perpetrator already accessed certain confidential information of the victim? Has the perpetrator's act resulted in severe bodily harm to the victim or his/her family members? Has the perpetrator continued to commit harm even after he has undergone a summary conviction? The court needs to see all these factors to consider whether the perpetrator may be considered as a simple offender, who may be subjected to a simple imprisonment and fine, or a habitual offender, or an offender who may still harbour revenge in his mind. Consider the cases of online sexual offences where the victim may not only feel threatened, but may also be the recipient of wrongdoing which threatens the well-being of the victim because of the privacy violation: for online non-consensual porn creation, the circulation-related offences, and especially video voyeurism, US legislation offers criminal and civil remedies, including fines and imprisonment.[41] Recently, in several states in the United States revenge porn laws have been introduced. These laws also prescribe fines and/or imprisonment as punishment.[42] In the United Kingdom, the offence of voyeurism is regulated by the newly introduced The *Voyeurism (Offences) Act* 2019 which prescribes a jail term for a minimum of 2 years.[43] Both in the United States and the United Kingdom the courts may also offer a no contact injunction and/or restriction orders if seen from the perspective of the laws mentioned in the above paragraphs. In Asian countries online sexual offences carry the heavy burden of shame for the victims. This is connected with an assumption of moral wrong, and hence the victim's participation in the commission of offence is almost always presumed.[44] Even though offences like voyeurism, creation, circulation of sexually explicit content, obscenity etc. result in punishment which may not be a summary conviction, but may include a jail term of 3 to 5 years, women victims may not feel comfortable in reporting such, fearing more harassment. However, in present times courts have begun to take a stricter preventive approach. Considering the fact that non-consensual pornography and revenge porn cases may not be considered felonies as per existing statutes, an English lower court in a recent judgement not only ordered restraint from committing further harm and publication of the victim's private photos and information and 'no contact' between the perpetrator and the victim, but the court also ordered the destruction of the phone of the perpetrator.[45] This course of action may not provide compete protection to the victim/s of revenge porn and/or non-consensual, non-consensual image sharing or even any other sort of offence that may violate the privacy of the victim by way of publishing private information, including images of the victim/s. However, it may provide temporary respite.[46]

As may be seen from the above discussion, such legislation primarily provides jail terms and fines: several researchers have opined that the State should also consider using the fined amount for repairing the damage to the reputation of the victims.[47] It may be noted that following the United States and the United Kingdom, several States, including Singapore, Philippines, Australia, Ghana, Pakistan, etc. have created laws for the preventive detention and fine of offenders of cyber-crimes, including interpersonal cyber-crimes. However, for the offence of child pornography, almost all laws in most jurisdictions have prescribed uniform punishment of a maximum of 10 to 20 years, depending upon the harm caused to the victim/s: these laws have been greatly influenced by the EU Convention on Cybercrime, 2001. Similarly, offences of online trafficking of drugs and weapons and human trafficking, including child, are also considered felonies which attract the heaviest jail terms, including life imprisonment.[48] As online trafficking falls within the meaning of organised crimes such as cyberterrorism, money laundering, etc., the penological approach focuses on preventive and deterrent approaches of punishment. Presently, several jurisdictions have also prescribed the registration of offenders under the sexual offender registry in order to label the offender for his life time.

6.3 Reformative and Therapeutic Jurisprudential Approaches to Cyber Penology

The above discussions may show that cyber-crime victimisation is deeply connected with human intelligence in operating computers and cyber technologies for the purpose of causing harm to the victims. Punishments may range from long-term imprisonment to summary convictions and/or fines or compensation to the victims, depending on the gravity of the offence. For terrorism, including cyberterrorism, States prefer to prescribe capital punishment in cases of grave violence to mankind. The penological trend in cyber-crime victimisation cases shows a reliance on restrictive, preventive, and reformative approaches in cases other than crimes of cyberterrorism. Penology for cyber offences is still growing. The legislature and the judiciary have emphasised civil and criminal remedies, including the no contact order, especially for interpersonal criminal activities. However, cyber-crime victimisation stands apart from physical crime victimisation in terms of the rapid expansion of victimisation: by the time the victim reports a cyber-crime, the police finish the investigation, and the courts finalise the conviction and punishments, the harm may have grown to a unthinkable degree to cause deep psychological and financial impact on the victim. This may happen even after the accused is arrested. Literally, the ball is put in motion and it snowballs, resulting in greater victimisation while the criminal justice machinery slowly takes action to analyse guilt and pronounce punishment. Often the police may concentrate on the perpetrator instead of his or her actions. It is still believed that once the preparator is arrested, the victimisation would stop. But this is not the case for cyber-crime victimisation cases. Unless the contents are taken down, the impact of victimisation continues to grow. Often this growth may not have any connection to the personal device of the offender: yet the criminal justice administration has to see the web platforms and the proxy offenders who knowingly or unknowingly cause more victimisation. Victims may not always be happy with the state-sanctioned punishments because there are possibilities of the offender returning under anonymity cloaks to carry out more harassment. In such instances, victims may prefer to opt for irrational coping methods like counter bullying, contacting amateur hackers, creating posts to

82 Penology for cyber victimisation

publicly shame the offender, etc.[49] States must consider enacting specific punishments for cyber offences so that the offenders may not plan, teach, or execute further offences from the prisons. The police must be trained to handle electronic evidences and devices so that the offenders may not be able to retrieve the offensive contents, images, etc. from the devices and data clouds.[50] In such cases, stakeholders are also moving to shift more of the burden to websites so that they assume their responsibility in preventing further harassment and remove the harassing content. The EU General Data Protection Regulation is a prime example in this respect. Courts on several occasions have indicated that websites should pay class compensation for data leaking, or for failing to take proper care when taking down offensive content, including risky online challenges like BlueWhale or MoMo. However, the tech giants like Facebook or Google need to be more victim friendly in the coming days.[51] The penological strategy for cyber-crime victimisation cases should be reformative for the offenders and therapeutic for the victims. Offenders may be prevented from accessing the internet for a specific period, publishing additional content about the victims, and contacting the victims and they may be asked to pay fines and compensation for repairing the financial loss the victims may undergo. They may even be made responsible for taking down certain offensive contents which may be within their reach, especially when the website requires the content to be removed by the uploader him/herself. But certain cases are beyond 'repairing,' even if the offender is arrested. Phishing cases are prime examples where victims may not regain the money unless their lawyers can prove that banks played a significant role in the monetary loss of the victims by way of negligence in strengthening customer care. Sexual offence cases and trolling also fall into the same category. Leaked personal images and insulting and defamatory comments may remain on the web space for a longer duration than expected. In such cases, the police and the courts need to expand punishment to the websites, including the dark net operators. Punishment, on the other hand needs to adhere to therapeutic jurisprudential approaches which may heal the victims. An apology and offer to repair the damage to reputation by the offender and his family must be considered as an inherent part of the sentence. Here, websites that fail to remove the contents must also be considered as offenders. But this must be executed in a manner which does not affect the privacy protection for the victim. It must be monitored by the probation officer assigned to the offender's case. Victim impact statements must particularly be given consideration in cyber-crime victimisation cases to measure the harm suffered by the victims. Revising the scope of the correctional administration system must be considered for juvenile and young offenders. Internet de-addiction may be of less help than counselling in the positive use of the internet. Similarly, the media and the State as a whole must stop glorifying juvenile offenders who are hackers and crackers. Such children must not be promoted by the State and/or companies for their hacking skills. This will serve no reformative purposes. Unless State parties consider introducing refined and revised cyber penology, victim justice for cyber-crime victimisation may not achieve its purpose.

Notes

1 Warr, M., Meier, R.F., & Erickson, M.L. (1983). Norms, theories of punishment, and publicly preferred penalties for crimes. *Sociological Quarterly, 24*(1), 75–91.
2 Wolfgag, M.E. (1965). Victim compensation in crimes of personal violence. *Minnesota Law Review, 50*, 223.; Cheeseman, H.R. (1980). Victim compensation: Law and economic analysis. *Hamline Law Review, 4*, 451.
3 For more information on this issue, see Blomberg, T.G., & Cohen, S. (Eds.). (2003). *Punishment and social control: New lines in criminology.* New York, NY: Transaction Publishers. ISBN: 0202307018, 9780202307015.
4 Ibid.
5 Feely M. & Jonathan S. *The new penology: Notes on the emerging strategy of corrections and its implications.* Available at https://scholarship.law.berkeley.edu/cgi/viewcontent.cgi?article=1717&context=facpubs. Accessed on 21.11.2019.

6 For example, see Savelsberg, J.J. (2018). Punitive turn and justice cascade: Mutual inspiration from punishment and society and human rights literatures. *Punishment & Society, 20*(1), 73–91. https://doi.org/10.1177/1462474517737049. Accessed on 21.12.2019.

7 Zehr, H., & Gohar, A. (2003). *The little book of restorative justice.* p. 21. Available at https://www.unicef.org/tdad/littlebookrjpakaf.pdf. Accessed on 12.12.2019.

8 Hawkins, D.J.B. (1944). Punishment and moral responsibility. *Modern Law Review*, 205–208. Published in https://onlinelibrary.wiley.com/doi/pdf/10.1111/j.1468-2230.1944.tb00984.x. Accessed on 12.12.2019.

9 Iyer, V.K. (1991). Bhoposhima: Crime without Punishment: Case for crisis management jurisprudence. *Economic and Political Weekly*, 2705–2713.

10 Ibid.

11 Wexler, D.B., & Winick, B.J. (1990). *Therapeutic jurisprudence: The law as a therapeutic agent.* Durham, NA: Carolina Academic Press. ISBN 978-0-89089-374-6.

12 Ibid.

13 Hoffman, M.B. (2001). Therapeutic jurisprudence, neo-rehabilitationism, and judicial collectivism: The least dangerous branch becomes most dangerous. *Fordham Urban Law Journal, 29*, 2063; Perlin, M.L. (2013). Yonder stands your orphan with his gun: The international human rights and therapeutic jurisprudence implications of juvenile punishment schemes. *Texas Technical Law Review, 46*, 301.

14 Halder, D., & Jaishankar. (2013). Revenge porn by teens in the United States and India: A socio-legal analysis. *International Annals of Criminology, 51*(1–2), 85–111. ISSN: 00034452; Halder, D. (2015). Cyber stalking victimisation of women: Evaluating the effectiveness of current laws in India from restorative justice and therapeutic, in jurisprudential perspectives. *Temida—The Journal on Victimization, Human Rights and Gender*, 103–130. ISSN: 1450–6637.

15 For greater understanding of this issue, see Collins, J.D., et al. (2011). Organizational data breaches 2005–2010: Applying SCP to the healthcare and education sectors. *International Journal of Cyber Criminology* (IJCC)*, 5*(1): 794–810. ISSN: 0974–2891.

16 S. 1030 18 U.S. Code (Fraud and related activity in connection with computers) says as follows:

a. Whoever—

1. having knowingly accessed a computer without authorization or exceeding authorized access, and by means of such conduct having obtained information that has been determined by the United States Government pursuant to an Executive order or statute to require protection against unauthorized disclosure for reasons of national defence or foreign relations, or any restricted data, as defined in paragraph y. of section 11 of the Atomic Energy Act of 1954, with reason to believe that such information so obtained could be used to the injury of the United States, or to the advantage of any foreign nation wilfully communicates, delivers, transmits, or causes to be communicated, delivered, or transmitted, or attempts to communicate, deliver, transmit or cause to be communicated, delivered, or transmitted the same to any person not entitled to receive it, or wilfully retains the same and fails to deliver it to the officer or employee of the United States entitled to receive it;

2. intentionally accesses a computer without authorization or exceeds authorized access, and thereby obtains—

   A. information contained in a financial record of a financial institution, or of a card issuer as defined in section 1602(n) [1] of title 15, or contained in a file of a consumer reporting agency on a consumer, as such terms are defined in the *Fair Credit Reporting Act* (15 U.S.C. 1681 et seq.);

   B. information from any department or agency of the United States; or

   C. information from any protected computer;

3. intentionally, without authorization to access any nonpublic computer of a department or agency of the United States, accesses such a computer of that department or agency that is exclusively for the use of the Government of the United States or, in the case of a computer not exclusively for such use, is used by or for the Government of the United States and such conduct affects that use by or for the Government of the United States;

4. knowingly and with intent to defraud, accesses a protected computer without authorization, or exceeds authorized access, and by means of such conduct furthers the intended fraud and obtains anything of value, unless the object of the fraud and the thing obtained consists only of the use of the computer and the value of such use is not more than $5,000 in any 1-year period;

84 Penology for cyber victimisation

5.

    A. knowingly causes the transmission of a program, information, code, or command, and as a result of such conduct, intentionally causes damage without authorization, to a protected computer;

    B. intentionally accesses a protected computer without authorization, and as a result of such conduct, recklessly causes damage; or

    C. intentionally accesses a protected computer without authorization, and as a result of such conduct, causes damage and loss [2].

6. knowingly and with intent to defraud traffics (as defined in section 1029) in any password or similar information through which a computer may be accessed without authorization, if—

    A. such trafficking affects interstate or foreign commerce; or

    B. such computer is used by or for the Government of the United States; [3]

7. with intent to extort from any person any money or other thing of value, transmits in interstate or foreign commerce any communication containing any—

    A. threat to cause damage to a protected computer;

    B. threat to obtain information from a protected computer without authorization or in excess of authorization or to impair the confidentiality of information obtained from a protected computer without authorization or by exceeding authorized access; or

    C. demand or request for money or other thing of value in relation to damage to a protected computer, where such damage was caused to facilitate the extortion

    shall be punished as provided in subsection (c) of this section.

17 S. 1030 18 U.S. Code (Fraud and related activity in connection with computers) in clause © speaks about the punishment and states as follows:

c. The punishment for an offense under subsection (a) or (b) of this section is—

1.

    A. a fine under this title or imprisonment for not more than ten years, or both, in the case of an offense under subsection (a)(1) of this section which does not occur after a conviction for another offense under this section, or an attempt to commit an offense punishable under this subparagraph; and

    B. a fine under this title or imprisonment for not more than twenty years, or both, in the case of an offense under subsection (a)(1) of this section which occurs after a conviction for another offense under this section, or an attempt to commit an offense punishable under this subparagraph;

2.

    A. except as provided in subparagraph (B), a fine under this title or imprisonment for not more than one year, or both, in the case of an offense under subsection (a)(2), (a)(3), or (a)(6) of this section which does not occur after a conviction for another offense under this section, or an attempt to commit an offense punishable under this subparagraph;

    B. a fine under this title or imprisonment for not more than 5 years, or both, in the case of an offense under subsection (a)(2), or an attempt to commit an offense punishable under this subparagraph, if—

        i. the offense was committed for purposes of commercial advantage or private financial gain;

        ii. the offense was committed in furtherance of any criminal or tortious act in violation of the Constitution or laws of the United States or of any State; or

        iii. the value of the information obtained exceeds $5,000; and

    D. a fine under this title or imprisonment for not more than ten years, or both, in the case of an offense under subsection (a)(2), (a)(3) or (a)(6) of this section which occurs after a conviction for another offense under this section, or an attempt to commit an offense punishable under this subparagraph;

3.

A. a fine under this title or imprisonment for not more than five years, or both, in the case of an offense under subsection (a)(4) or (a)(7) of this section which does not occur after a conviction for another offense under this section, or an attempt to commit an offense punishable under this subparagraph; and

B. a fine under this title or imprisonment for not more than ten years, or both, in the case of an offense under subsection (a)(4),[4] or (a)(7) of this section which occurs after a conviction for another offense under this section, or an attempt to commit an offense punishable under this subparagraph;

4.

A. except as provided in subparagraphs (E) and (F), a fine under this title, imprisonment for not more than 5 years, or both, in the case of—

i. an offense under subsection (a)(5)(B), which does not occur after a conviction for another offense under this section, if the offense caused (or, in the case of an attempted offense, would, if completed, have caused)—

I. loss to 1 or more persons during any 1-year period (and, for purposes of an investigation, prosecution, or other proceeding brought by the United States only, loss resulting from a related course of conduct affecting 1 or more other protected computers) aggregating at least $5,000 in value;

II. the modification or impairment, or potential modification or impairment, of the medical examination, diagnosis, treatment, or care of 1 or more individuals;

III. physical injury to any person;

IV. a threat to public health or safety;

V. damage affecting a computer used by or for an entity of the United States Government in furtherance of the administration of justice, national defence, or national security; or

VI. damage affecting 10 or more protected computers during any 1-year period; or

ii. an attempt to commit an offense punishable under this subparagraph;

B. except as provided in subparagraphs (E) and (F), a fine under this title, imprisonment for not more than 10 years, or both, in the case of—

i. an offense under subsection (a)(5)(A), which does not occur after a conviction for another offense under this section, if the offense caused (or, in the case of an attempted offense, would, if completed, have caused) a harm provided in subclauses (I) through (VI) of subparagraph (A)(i); or

ii. an attempt to commit an offense punishable under this subparagraph;

C. except as provided in subparagraphs (E) and (F), a fine under this title, imprisonment for not more than 20 years, or both, in the case of—

i. an offense or an attempt to commit an offense under subparagraphs (A) or (B) of subsection (a)(5) that occurs after a conviction for another offense under this section; or

ii. an attempt to commit an offense punishable under this subparagraph;

D. a fine under this title, imprisonment for not more than 10 years, or both, in the case of—

i. an offense or an attempt to commit an offense under subsection (a)(5)(C) that occurs after a conviction for another offense under this section; or

ii. an attempt to commit an offense punishable under this subparagraph;

E. if the offender attempts to cause or knowingly or recklessly causes serious bodily injury from conduct in violation of subsection (a)(5)(A), a fine under this title, imprisonment for not more than 20 years, or both;

F. if the offender attempts to cause or knowingly or recklessly causes death from conduct in violation of subsection (a)(5)(A), a fine under this title, imprisonment for any term of years or for life, or both; or

86 Penology for cyber victimisation

    G. a fine under this title, imprisonment for not more than 1 year, or both, for—

        i. any other offense under subsection (a)(5); or
        ii. an attempt to commit an offense punishable under this subparagraph.

d.

1. The United States Secret Service shall, in addition to any other agency having such authority, have the authority to investigate offenses under this section.
2. The Federal Bureau of Investigation shall have primary authority to investigate offenses under subsection (a)(1) for any cases involving espionage, foreign counterintelligence, information protected against unauthorized disclosure for reasons of national defence or foreign relations, or Restricted Data (as that term is defined in section 11y of the Atomic Energy Act of 1954 (42 U.S.C. 2014(y)), except for offenses affecting the duties of the United States Secret Service pursuant to section 3056(a) of this title.
3. Such authority shall be exercised in accordance with an agreement which shall be entered into by the Secretary of the Treasury and the Attorney General.

e. As used in this section—

1. the term "computer" means an electronic, magnetic, optical, electrochemical, or other high speed data processing device performing logical, arithmetic, or storage functions, and includes any data storage facility or communications facility directly related to or operating in conjunction with such device, but such term does not include an automated typewriter or typesetter, a portable hand held calculator, or other similar device;
2. the term "protected computer" means a computer—

    A. exclusively for the use of a financial institution or the United States Government, or, in the case of a computer not exclusively for such use, used by or for a financial institution or the United States Government and the conduct constituting the offense affects that use by or for the financial institution or the Government; or
    B. which is used in or affecting interstate or foreign commerce or communication, including a computer located outside the United States that is used in a manner that affects interstate or foreign commerce or communication of the United States;

3. the term "State" includes the District of Columbia, the Commonwealth of Puerto Rico, and any other commonwealth, possession or territory of the United States;
4. the term "financial institution" means—

    A. an institution, with deposits insured by the Federal Deposit Insurance Corporation;
    B. the Federal Reserve or a member of the Federal Reserve including any Federal Reserve Bank;
    C. a credit union with accounts insured by the National Credit Union Administration;
    D. a member of the Federal home loan bank system and any home loan bank;
    E. any institution of the Farm Credit System under the Farm Credit Act of 1971;
    F. a broker-dealer registered with the Securities and Exchange Commission pursuant to section 15 of the Securities Exchange Act of 1934;
    G. the Securities Investor Protection Corporation;
    H. a branch or agency of a foreign bank (as such terms are defined in paragraphs (1) and (3) of section 1(b) of the International Banking Act of 1978); and
    I. an organization operating under section 25 or section 25(a) 1 of the Federal Reserve Act;

5. the term "financial record" means information derived from any record held by a financial institution pertaining to a customer's relationship with the financial institution;
6. the term "exceeds authorized access" means to access a computer with authorization and to use such access to obtain or alter information in the computer that the accessor is not entitled so to obtain or alter;
7. the term "department of the United States" means the legislative or judicial branch of the Government or one of the executive departments enumerated in section 101 of title 5;
8. the term "damage" means any impairment to the integrity or availability of data, a program, a system, or information;

9. the term "government entity" includes the Government of the United States, any State or political subdivision of the United States, any foreign country, and any state, province, municipality, or other political subdivision of a foreign country;

10. the term "conviction" shall include a conviction under the law of any State for a crime punishable by imprisonment for more than 1 year, an element of which is unauthorized access, or exceeding authorized access, to a computer;

11. the term "loss" means any reasonable cost to any victim, including the cost of responding to an offense, conducting a damage assessment, and restoring the data, program, system, or information to its condition prior to the offense, and any revenue lost, cost incurred, or other consequential damages incurred because of interruption of service; and

12. the term "person" means any individual, firm, corporation, educational institution, financial institution, governmental entity, or legal or other entity.

f. This section does not prohibit any lawfully authorized investigative, protective, or intelligence activity of a law enforcement agency of the United States, a State, or a political subdivision of a State, or of an intelligence agency of the United States.

g. Any person who suffers damage or loss by reason of a violation of this section may maintain a civil action against the violator to obtain compensatory damages and injunctive relief or other equitable relief. A civil action for a violation of this section may be brought only if the conduct involves 1 of the factors set forth in subclauses [5] (I), (II), (III), (IV), or (V) of subsection (c)(4)(A)(i). Damages for a violation involving only conduct described in subsection (c)(4)(A)(i)(I) are limited to economic damages. No action may be brought under this subsection unless such action is begun within 2 years of the date of the act complained of or the date of the discovery of the damage. No action may be brought under this subsection for the negligent design or manufacture of computer hardware, computer software, or firmware.

h. The Attorney General and the Secretary of the Treasury shall report to the Congress annually, during the first 3 years following the date of the enactment of this subsection, concerning investigations and prosecutions under subsection (a)(5).

i.

1. The court, in imposing sentence on any person convicted of a violation of this section, or convicted of conspiracy to violate this section, shall order, in addition to any other sentence imposed and irrespective of any provision of State law, that such person forfeit to the United States—

   A. such person's interest in any personal property that was used or intended to be used to commit or to facilitate the commission of such violation; and
   B. any property, real or personal, constituting or derived from, any proceeds that such person obtained, directly or indirectly, as a result of such violation.

2. The criminal forfeiture of property under this subsection, any seizure and disposition thereof, and any judicial proceeding in relation thereto, shall be governed by the provisions of section 413 of the Comprehensive Drug Abuse Prevention and Control Act of 1970 (21 U.S.C. 853), except subsection (d) of that section.

j. For purposes of subsection (i), the following shall be subject to forfeiture to the United States and no property right shall exist in them:

1. Any personal property used or intended to be used to commit or to facilitate the commission of any violation of this section, or a conspiracy to violate this section.
2. Any property, real or personal, which constitutes or is derived from proceeds traceable to any violation of this section, or a conspiracy to violate this section.

18 Ibid.
19 See https://www.law.cornell.edu/uscode/text/18/1030. Accessed on 21.12.2019.
20 For more information, see the *Official Secrets Act*, 1911.
21 For example, consider the *Official Secrets Act*, 1911.
22 See Understanding the Cybersecurity of America's aviation sector: Joint hearing before the subcommittee on cybersecurity and infrastructure protection and the subcommittee on transportation and protective security of the Committee on Homeland Security held on September 6, 2018. Available at

https://www.govinfo.gov/content/pkg/CHRG-115hhrg34446/html/CHRG-115hhrg34446.htm. Accessed on 12.12.2020.

23 Wachtel, H.A. (2005). Targeting Osama Bin Laden: Examining the legality of assassination as a tool of US foreign policy. *Duke Law Journal, 55*(3), 677–710.

24 Halder, D. (2011). *Information Technology Act* and Cyber terrorism: A critical review. In P.M.S. Sundaram & S. Umarhathab (Eds.), *Cyber crime and digital disorder* (pp. 75–90). Tirunelveli, India: Publication Division, Manonmaniam Sundaranar University. ISBN: 9789381402191.

25 Ibid.

26 For example, see PTI (2021) US allows Tahawwur to file additional reply in extradition case to India. Published in https://www.business-standard.com/article/current-affairs/us-allows-tahawwur-to-file-additional-reply-in-extradition-case-to-india-121040100331_1.html on April 1, 2021. Accessed on 02-04-2021.

27 After the 26/11 attack, India also revamped its laws regarding cyber terrorism. The *Information Technology Act*, 2000 (amended in 2008) prescribes capital punishment as the maximum punishment for cyber terrorism under S.66F.

28 This case is discussed in Chapter 5 of this book.

29 Hinduja, S., & Patchin, J.W. (2010). Cyberbullying research center. Available at http://www.shawnedgington.com/resources/bullying-and-cyberbullying-laws/. Accessed on 12.12.2020. Retrieved February, 3, 2011; El Asam, A., & Samara, M. (2016). Cyberbullying and the law: A review of psychological and legal challenges. *Computers in Human Behavior, 65*, 127–141; Young, H., Campbell, M., Spears, B., Butler, D., Cross, D., & Slee, P. (2016). Cyberbullying and the role of the law in Australian schools: Views of senior officials. *Australian Journal of Education, 60*(1), 86–101; Marcum, C.D., & Higgins, G.E. (2019). Examining the effectiveness of academic scholarship on the fight against cyberbullying and cyberstalking. *American Journal of Criminal Justice, 44*(4), 645–655.

30 Ibid.

31 Citron, D K. (2014). *Hate crimes in cyberspace*. Harvard University Press.

32 *Caplan v Atas*, 2021 ONSC 670.

33 Ibid.

34 S.2A of this provision is noteworthy here which says as follows:

2A Offence of stalking

1. A person is guilty of an offence if—

   a. the person pursues a course of conduct in breach of section 1(1), and
   b. the course of conduct amounts to stalking.

2. For the purposes of subsection (1)(b) (and section 4A(1)(a)) a person's course of conduct amounts to stalking of another person if—

   a. it amounts to harassment of that person,
   b. the acts or omissions involved are ones associated with stalking, and
   c. the person whose course of conduct it is knows or ought to know that the course of conduct amounts to harassment of the other person.

3. The following are examples of acts or omissions which, in particular circumstances, are ones associated with stalking—

   a. following a person,
   b. contacting, or attempting to contact, a person by any means,
   c. publishing any statement or other material—

      i. relating or purporting to relate to a person, or
      ii. purporting to originate from a person,

   d. monitoring the use by a person of the internet, email or any other form of electronic communication,
   e. loitering in any place (whether public or private),
   f. interfering with any property in the possession of a person,
   g. watching or spying on a person.

4. A person guilty of an offence under this section is liable on summary conviction to imprisonment for a term not exceeding 51 weeks, or a fine not exceeding level 5 on the standard scale, or both.

Penology for cyber victimisation **89**

5. In relation to an offence committed before the commencement of section 281(5) of the Criminal Justice Act 2003, the reference in subsection (4) to 51 weeks is to be read as a reference to six months

35 See Halder D., & Jaishankar, K. (2012). *Cyber crime and the victimization of women: Laws, rights, and regulations.* Hershey, PA: IGI Global. ISBN: 978-1-60960-830-9.
36 See S.2261B of US Code 18.
37 S.354D of the Indian Penal Code states as follows:

1. Any man who follows a woman and contacts, or attempts to contact such woman to foster personal interaction repeatedly despite a clear indication of disinterest by such woman; or monitors the use by a woman of the internet, email or any other form of electronic communication, commits the offence of stalking; Provided that such conduct shall not amount to stalking if the man who pursued it proves that—it was pursued for the purpose of preventing or detecting crime and the man accused of stalking had been entrusted with the responsibility of prevention and detection of crime by the State; or it was pursued under any law or to comply with any condition or requirement imposed by any person under any law; or in the particular circumstances such conduct was reasonable and justified.
2. Whoever commits the offence of stalking shall be punished on first conviction with imprisonment of either description for a term which may extend to three years, and shall also be liable to fine; and be punished on a second or subsequent conviction, with imprisonment of either description for a term which may extend to five years, and shall also be liable to fine.

Also see Halder, D. (2015). Cyber stalking victimisation of women: Evaluating the effectiveness of current laws in India from restorative justice and therapeutic, in jurisprudential perspectives. *Temida—The Journal on Victimization, Human Rights and Gender*, pp.103–130. ISSN: 1450–6637.
38 See Halder D. (2015). Cyber stalking victimisation of women: Evaluating the effectiveness of current laws in India from restorative justice and therapeutic, in jurisprudential perspectives. *Temida—The Journal on Victimization, Human Rights and Gender*, 103–130. ISSN: 1450–6637.
39 Ibid.
40 18 U.S. Code § 1028 states as follows: (a)Whoever, in a circumstance described in subsection (c) of this section—

1. knowingly and without lawful authority produces an identification document, authentication feature, or a false identification document;
2. knowingly transfers an identification document, authentication feature, or a false identification document knowing that such document or feature was stolen or produced without lawful authority;
3. knowingly possesses with intent to use unlawfully or transfer unlawfully five or more identification documents (other than those issued lawfully for the use of the possessor), authentication features, or false identification documents;
4. knowingly possesses an identification document (other than one issued lawfully for the use of the possessor), authentication feature, or a false identification document, with the intent such document or feature be used to defraud the United States;
5. knowingly produces, transfers, or possesses a document-making implement or authentication feature with the intent such document-making implement or authentication feature will be used in the production of a false identification document or another document-making implement or authentication feature which will be so used;
6. knowingly possesses an identification document or authentication feature that is or appears to be an identification document or authentication feature of the United States or a sponsoring entity of an event designated as a special event of national significance which is stolen or produced without lawful authority knowing that such document or feature was stolen or produced without such authority;
7. knowingly transfers, possesses, or uses, without lawful authority, a means of identification of another person with the intent to commit, or to aid or abet, or in connection with, any unlawful activity that constitutes a violation of Federal law, or that constitutes a felony under any applicable State or local law; or

90 Penology for cyber victimisation

8. knowingly traffics in false or actual authentication features for use in false identification documents, document-making implements, or means of identification; shall be punished as provided in subsection (b) of this section.

b. The punishment for an offense under subsection (a) of this section is—

1. except as provided in paragraphs (3) and (4), a fine under this title or imprisonment for not more than 15 years, or both, if the offense is—

   A. the production or transfer of an identification document, authentication feature, or false identification document that is or appears to be—

      i. an identification document or authentication feature issued by or under the authority of the United States; or
      ii. a birth certificate, or a driver's license or personal identification card;

   B. the production or transfer of more than five identification documents, authentication features, or false identification documents;
   C. an offense under paragraph (5) of such subsection; or
   D. an offense under paragraph (7) of such subsection that involves the transfer, possession, or use of 1 or more means of identification if, as a result of the offense, any individual committing the offense obtains anything of value aggregating $1,000 or more during any 1-year period;

2. except as provided in paragraphs (3) and (4), a fine under this title or imprisonment for not more than 5 years, or both, if the offense is—

   A. any other production, transfer, or use of a means of identification, an identification document,[1] authentication feature, or a false identification document; or
   B. an offense under paragraph (3) or (7) of such subsection;

3. a fine under this title or imprisonment for not more than 20 years, or both, if the offense is committed—

   A. to facilitate a drug trafficking crime (as defined in section 929(a)(2));
   B. in connection with a crime of violence (as defined in section 924(c)(3)); or
   C. after a prior conviction under this section becomes final;

4. a fine under this title or imprisonment for not more than 30 years, or both, if the offense is committed to facilitate an act of domestic terrorism (as defined under section 2331(5) of this title) or an act of international terrorism (as defined in section 2331(1) of this title);

5. in the case of any offense under subsection (a), forfeiture to the United States of any personal property used or intended to be used to commit the offense; and
6. a fine under this title or imprisonment for not more than one year, or both, in any other case.

c. The circumstance referred to in subsection (a) of this section is that—

1. the identification document, authentication feature, or false identification document is or appears to be issued by or under the authority of the United States or a sponsoring entity of an event designated as a special event of national significance or the document-making implement is designed or suited for making such an identification document, authentication feature, or false identification document;
2. the offense is an offense under subsection (a)(4) of this section; or
3. either—

   A. the production, transfer, possession, or use prohibited by this section is in or affects interstate or foreign commerce, including the transfer of a document by electronic means; or
   B. the means of identification, identification document, false identification document, or document-making implement is transported in the mail in the course of the production, transfer, possession, or use prohibited by this section.

d. In this section and section 1028A—

1. the term "authentication feature" means any hologram, watermark, certification, symbol, code, image, sequence of numbers or letters, or other feature that either individually or in combination with another feature is used by the issuing authority on an identification document, document-making implement, or means of identification to determine if the document is counterfeit, altered, or otherwise falsified;

2. the term "document-making implement" means any implement, impression, template, computer file, computer disc, electronic device, or computer hardware or software, that is specifically configured or primarily used for making an identification document, a false identification document, or another document-making implement;

3. the term "identification document" means a document made or issued by or under the authority of the United States Government, a State, political subdivision of a State, a sponsoring entity of an event designated as a special event of national significance, a foreign government, political subdivision of a foreign government, an international governmental or an international quasi-governmental organization which, when completed with information concerning a particular individual, is of a type intended or commonly accepted for the purpose of identification of individuals;

4. the term "false identification document" means a document of a type intended or commonly accepted for the purposes of identification of individuals that—

    A. is not issued by or under the authority of a governmental entity or was issued under the authority of a governmental entity but was subsequently altered for purposes of deceit; and

    B. appears to be issued by or under the authority of the United States Government, a State, a political subdivision of a State, a sponsoring entity of an event designated by the President as a special event of national significance, a foreign government, a political subdivision of a foreign government, or an international governmental or quasi-governmental organization;

5. the term "false authentication feature" means an authentication feature that—

    A. is genuine in origin, but, without the authorization of the issuing authority, has been tampered with or altered for purposes of deceit;

    B. is genuine, but has been distributed, or is intended for distribution, without the authorization of the issuing authority and not in connection with a lawfully made identification document, document-making implement, or means of identification to which such authentication feature is intended to be affixed or embedded by the respective issuing authority; or

    C. appears to be genuine, but is not;

6. the term "issuing authority"—

    A. means any governmental entity or agency that is authorized to issue identification documents, means of identification, or authentication features; and

    B. includes the United States Government, a State, a political subdivision of a State, a sponsoring entity of an event designated by the President as a special event of national significance, a foreign government, a political subdivision of a foreign government, or an international government or quasi-governmental organization;

7. the term "means of identification" means any name or number that may be used, alone or in conjunction with any other information, to identify a specific individual, including any—

    A. name, social security number, date of birth, official State or government issued driver's license or identification number, alien registration number, government passport number, employer or taxpayer identification number;

    B. unique biometric data, such as fingerprint, voice print, retina or iris image, or other unique physical representation;

    C. unique electronic identification number, address, or routing code; or

    D. telecommunication identifying information or access device (as defined in section 1029(e));

92 Penology for cyber victimisation

8. the term "personal identification card" means an identification document issued by a State or local government solely for the purpose of identification;
9. the term "produce" includes alter, authenticate, or assemble;
10. the term "transfer" includes selecting an identification document, false identification document, or document-making implement and placing or directing the placement of such identification document, false identification document, or document-making implement on an online location where it is available to others;
11. the term "State" includes any State of the United States, the District of Columbia, the Commonwealth of Puerto Rico, and any other commonwealth, possession, or territory of the United States; and
12. the term "traffic" means—

   A. to transport, transfer, or otherwise dispose of, to another, as consideration for anything of value; or
   B. to make or obtain control of with intent to so transport, transfer, or otherwise dispose of.

e. This section does not prohibit any lawfully authorized investigative, protective, or intelligence activity of a law enforcement agency of the United States, a State, or a political subdivision of a State, or of an intelligence agency of the United States, or any activity authorized under chapter 224 of this title.

f. Attempt and Conspiracy.—

Any person who attempts or conspires to commit any offense under this section shall be subject to the same penalties as those prescribed for the offense, the commission of which was the object of the attempt or conspiracy.

g. Forfeiture Procedures.—

The forfeiture of property under this section, including any seizure and disposition of the property and any related judicial or administrative proceeding, shall be governed by the provisions of section 413 (other than subsection (d) of that section) of the Comprehensive Drug Abuse Prevention and Control Act of 1970 (21 U.S.C. 853).

h. Forfeiture; Disposition.—

In the circumstance in which any person is convicted of a violation of subsection (a), the court shall order, in addition to the penalty prescribed, the forfeiture and destruction or other disposition of all illicit authentication features, identification documents, document-making implements, or means of identification.

i. Rule of Construction.—

For purpose of subsection (a)(7), a single identification document or false identification document that contains 1 or more means of identification shall be construed to be 1 means of identification.

41 for example, see 18 U.S. Code § 1801 which speaks about Video voyeurism and says as follows:

a. Whoever, in the special maritime and territorial jurisdiction of the United States, has the intent to capture an image of a private area of an individual without their consent, and knowingly does so under circumstances in which the individual has a reasonable expectation of privacy, shall be fined under this title or imprisoned not more than one year, or both.

b. In this section—

1. the term "capture," with respect to an image, means to videotape, photograph, film, record by any means, or broadcast;
2. the term "broadcast" means to electronically transmit a visual image with the intent that it be viewed by a person or persons;
3. the term "a private area of the individual" means the naked or undergarment clad genitals, pubic area, buttocks, or female breast of that individual;
4. the term "female breast" means any portion of the female breast below the top of the areola; and

5. the term "under circumstances in which that individual has a reasonable expectation of privacy" means—

    A. circumstances in which a reasonable person would believe that he or she could disrobe in privacy, without being concerned that an image of a private area of the individual was being captured; or

    B. circumstances in which a reasonable person would believe that a private area of the individual would not be visible to the public, regardless of whether that person is in a public or private place.

    C. This section does not prohibit any lawful law enforcement, correctional, or intelligence activity.

42 For more information, see https://www.cybercivilrights.org/revenge-porn-laws/. Accessed on 12.12.2019.

43 For more information, see https://www.gov.uk/government/publications/implementation-of-the-voyeurism-offences-act-2019. Accessed on 12.12.2019.

44 For a greater understanding of this issue, see 15. Halder, D., & Jaishankar, K. (2015). Irrational coping theory and positive criminology: A frame work to protect victims of cyber crime. In N. Ronel and D. Segev (Eds.), *Positive criminology* (pp. 276–291). Abingdon, Oxon: Routledge. ISBN: 978-0-415-74856-8.

45 See BBC (2021) Judge calls for higher court to rule on revenge porn. Published in https://www.bbc.com/news/uk-northern-ireland-56085409 on 16-02-2021. Accessed on 16-02-2021.

46 For example, in India, voyeurism is dealt with by S.354C of the Indian Penal Code which says as follows:

> Any man who watches, or captures the image of a woman engaging in a private act in circumstances where she would usually have the expectation of not being observed either by the perpetrator or by any other person at the behest of the perpetrator or disseminates such image shall be punished on first conviction with imprisonment of either description for a term which shall not be less than one year, but which may extend to three years, and shall also be liable to fine, and be punished on a second or subsequent conviction, with imprisonment of either description for a term which shall not be less than three years, but which may extend to seven years, and shall also be liable to fine.

Similar sentences are also available in Bangladesh, Pakistan etc. For more detail, see Halder, D. (2017). Revenge porn against women and the applicability of therapeutic jurisprudence: A comparative analysis of regulations in India, Pakistan and Bangladesh. In D. Halder & K. Jaishankar (Eds.), *Therapeutic jurisprudence and overcoming violence against women.* IGI Global. ISSN: 2475–6644.

47 For example, see Halder, D., & Jaishankar, K. (2016). *Cyber crimes against women in India.* New Delhi: SAGE Publications. ISBN: 9789385985775; Citron, D.K. (2014). *Hate crimes in cyberspace.* Cambridge, MA: Harvard University Press. ISBN: 978-0-674-36829-3.

48 For example, consider 18 U.S.C. § 1591, which prescribes a minimum 10 years of imprisonment to maximum life imprisonment for child sex trafficking. Also see Dixon, H.B., Jr. (2013). Human trafficking and the internet (and other technologies, too). *The Judges Journal, 52,* 36.

49 For a greater understanding of this issue, see 15. Halder, D., & Jaishankar, K. (2015). Irrational coping theory and positive criminology: A frame work to protect victims of cyber crime. In N. Ronel and D. Segev (Eds.), *Positive criminology* (pp. 276–291). Abingdon, Oxon: Routledge. ISBN: 978-0-415-74856-8.

50 For more detail, see Halder D., & Jaishankar, K. (2016). *Cyber crimes against women in India.* New Delhi: SAGE Publications. ISBN: 9789385985775.

51 See 8. Halder, D. (2018). The #BlueWhale challenge to the Indian judiciary: A critical analysis of the response of the Indian higher judiciary to risky online contents with special reference to BlueWhale Suicide game. In T. Sourdin & A. Zariski (Eds.), *The responsive judges* (pp. 256–276). New York, NY: Springer.

7
CONCLUSION

Patterns of online victimisation are ever expanding. Victimological analysis of such growth is necessary now more than ever. The millennium had seen the creation of numerous laws and policy guidelines to criminalise and punish a number of forms of cyber-crime victimisation. Earlier, it was assumed that cyberspace is not regulable because of the issues of jurisdiction and anonymity. However, in more recent years law researchers made it clear that the internet can be regulable provided that state parties collaborate with each other to allow investigations in their jurisdictions, the apprehension of criminals, and the initiation of judicial probes. International stakeholders, including the UN bodies, invited governmental and non-governmental agencies and organisations, individual researchers, and web companies to formulate principles that would be considered as Conventions. These international stakeholders invited state parties to form treaties on the basis of such conventions so that the recognition of offences may be universal. Simultaneously, state parties and international stakeholders encouraged research to understand emerging patterns of victimisation, who the perpetrators were, why they were committing such crimes, what their modus operandi was, and how they were using cyberspace to access victims. In the 1990s Laurence Lessig suggested that cyberspace activities had a huge market and this market continues to grow today. It can be well managed for positive and negative gains, and laws need to be created to address such issues. By 2001, the United States became the biggest victim of terrorism, including cyberterrorism. This was the period when the State's vulnerability as a victim began to attract notice. While on the one hand terror organisations rapidly started expanding their online networks, on the other hand, the demand for the dark web waned. This secret channel of communication no longer remained a treasured source of information for the US military. The dark web became a vicious illegal marketplace for criminal ideas, illegal weapons, drugs, and illegal porn content. Since 2004, social media companies have grown rapidly. They became the people's place to socialise. The companies started earning huge profits because of advertisements. But what they did not notice was the terror organisations' operations on their platforms. Web companies practically ran parallel governance: they had their own rules, policies, content removing guidelines, and the battalions of engineers and policy strategists who would decide which content should be removed, which profiles should be provided anonymity cloaks, and which information should not be shared with the government. This encouraged activists and perpetrators to take refuge in the web world. In between, state parties rapidly adopted e-governance strategies for improving public welfare and facilitating better access of

DOI: 10.4324/9781315155685-7

public facilities, banking services, and justice for the public. Government agencies not only had their own websites, they also created social media handles to conduct better public reach. But this invited more trouble. Soon the internet became a conduit of criminal activities. Perpetrators could now identify their victims sooner than ever before. The price of the private data also soured in the market: a hospital can be hacked with a ransom threat because the perpetrators know that leaking of health data may cause millions of people to lose their job, feel embarrassed in public, or have their personal lives badly affected. Perpetrators also know that accessing the health information of adults may victimise their children as well. Both the hospital and its patients can become the victims of cyber-crimes, but in different capacities. Perpetrators hack schools and childcare institutions to extract data and images of children. This material would fetch them profit in two ways: they could make ransom demands to the institutes and also sell the profiles and the images of children to the porn market. Young men and women who may face economic challenges in the job market are quickly turning to the internet to make money, both in ethical and unethical ways. People are creating millions of apps for their own businesses, which store private data of many others. Users/subscribers/customers are facing security challenges in cyberspace. But the internet has become such an integral part of our lives that we cannot think of doing without these little smart devices.

It is important to now understand why States, organisations, and individuals become victimised in cyberspace. Even if the laws have prescribed punishments for cyber offences, it is evident that such punishments have failed to create deterrence in the minds of people. Victims are asked embarrassing questions at the police office or prosecution office, and there is widespread media speculation about specific classes of victims. This results in the victims staying silent. This also results in victims deciding to take the law in their own hands and to try irrational coping mechanisms, only to make the situation worse. Unlike physical crime victimisation, courts have not yet looked at victim impact statements in cases of cyber-crime victimisation. In certain cases, the impact of cyber-victimisation is widely visible because of the mass destruction of lives and properties in physical space. But in other cases, where the victims are ordinary individuals, the impact is almost always intangible. Cyber Victimology as a discipline may help to improve this situation. It may help the criminal justice system as a whole to recognise the rights of victims of cyber-crimes. It may also help towards the restoration of justice by application of Therapeutic Jurisprudence for determining punishments and for determining how to provide victim assistance by front-line professionals. This may necessarily help improve the victim assistance system, which may then lead to positive gain for the victims. This book discusses the issue of digital empowerment of victims of cyber-crimes to gain better access to justice. State parties need to develop their legal infrastructure and cybersecurity infrastructure in a victim-friendly manner. Victim justice also includes protection of witnesses and victims. State parties and international stakeholders must ensure that victims of cyber-crimes are prevented and protected from repeat victimisation that may occur due to anger and the vengeful outlooks of the offender/s. Further, their data must be protected from further exploitation. Improving victim justice would necessarily mean training the victim assistants in dealing with unknown and unthinkable challenges in cyberspace. In this goal, intermediaries, tech companies, and web companies must be actively included. They must provide better security mechanisms for preventing the escalation of known offences and the occurrence of new patterns of offences. This book has suggested that state-parties and international stakeholders must consider applying machine intelligence to detect probable criminal gangs and criminal behaviours in cyberspace and the types of vulnerable data that may attract criminals. Awareness-building should continue in order to prevent the victimisation of specific classes of victims. But the effect of such awareness must also be continuously updated. Victims of cyber-crimes need to be heard to understand where States are failing in order to prevent continued victimisation.

This book was prepared during a time when dependency on the internet, e-banking, the-education system, and machine intelligence had skyrocketed due to Covid-19 restrictions. This period saw a steep growth in cyber victimisation cases and the use of cyberspace for spreading fake news and rumours, and making threats in general. This period showed how cyberspace remains a potent source of victimisation. It is hoped that the concept of Cyber Victimology may be considered by all stakeholders to improve the plight of victims and that the subject may be enriched with further research, which may be beneficial for victims around the globe.

GLOSSARY

Advance scam: Fraudulently extracting money from the victim over information and digital communication technology by way of making the victim believe that the amount would be necessary to obtain a gift or property in real life.

Artificial intelligence: Computer programs containing human intelligence that will enable the machine to presume its function and execute the same efficiently with the help of algorithms and human intelligence that may operate such programs.

Child online sexual materials: Creation of sexually explicit contents and sharing the same in cyberspace by using data and images of children illegally and unauthorisedly for unethical gains.

Cyberbullying: Using harsh, insulting, and humiliating words and images to create comments in cyberspace to insult and annoy others.

Cyber-crimes: Crimes committed in cyberspace, with the aid of information and digital technology.

Cyber-crime victims: Those individuals/organizations who have been victimized in cyberspace by different patterns of cyber-crimes and who may have lost money due to such victimisation, or who may have suffered reputation damage, or who may have been victimised due to the creation of pornographic contents, including revenge porn contents.

Cyberspace: An abstract virtual space created with the help of internet and digital communication technology that facilitates information and data creation, exchange, and storage.

Cyber stalking: Intentionally monitoring someone over cyberspace to gain information about the said person and to create a threat in the mind of that person.

Cyberterrorism: Using cyberspace for conducting terror activities, which may have devastating effects in real life.

Cyber victimology: Study of the causation of victimisation, pattern of victimisation and victimhood, impact of victimisation and the treatment of victims of cyber-crimes.

Data: Any specific information stored in the computer in a specific manner.

Intermediary: Any individual or organisation that may facilitate information exchange, communication with other others, and creation of contents on web platforms and which may store and process data.

98 Glossary

Job scam: Fraudulently gaining money by deceiving an individual/group of individuals with fake promises for jobs by using information and communication technology.

Online defamation: Sharing false, unwanted information of one to other/s through information and digital communication technology to cause insult and embarrassment.

Revenge porn: Gratification of revenge over the victim by way of creating porn contents with the personal information and images of the victim and sharing the same to the worldwide audience without proper consent.

Therapeutic jurisprudence: A specific school of jurisprudence which uses law as a healing tool for helping victims to recover from trauma, which helps in reformation of the offenders and works towards restoration of justice holistically.

INDEX

Abbottabad 76
Adriano, E.A.Q. 37
advance fee scams 19, 23, 50, 64
Al Qaeda 76
ancient Indian scripts 1
anonymity 10
anonymous veil 16
Anti-Child Pornography Act of 2009 68
Anticybersquatting Consumer Protection Act (1999) 21
anti-cyberstalking law 79
Anti-Trafficking in Persons Act of 2003 68
Apple 13
Arab Spring in early 2010 24
Arthashashtra 1
artificial intelligence 8, 19, 43, 48, 55, 65
Assange, J. 54
assassination 76
assistance for cyber-crime victims 61–63
Atomic Energy Act of 1954 31n31, 83n16
Attorney General and the Secretary of the Treasury 87n17
awareness-building 95

Basic Principles and Guidelines on the Right to a Remedy and Reparation for Victims of Gross Violations of International Human Rights Law and Serious Violations of International Humanitarian Law, 2005 (2005 Guidelines) 4, 8, 58, 60, 61
Black Tigers 14
BlueWhale 82
bodily privacy, infringement of 25
British Airways 18, 33n44
Budapest Convention 14, 36, 47, 49, 53, 55, 57, 61
bullying 22
Button, M. 47

Caliphet 15
Cambridge Analytica (2015) 66
capital punishment 74, 77
Caplan v. Atas (2021) 67, 72n66, 78
Centre for Cyber Victim Counselling (CCVC) 63
child pornography 43, 49, 51, 81
children: home-quarantined 5; online sexual exploitation 25; as victims of cyber-crimes 29
Child's Play case 50
child trafficking 25, 43, 50
Citron, D K. 78
civil aviation computer infrastructure 6
civil society organisations 63
Code of Hammurabi 1
communication; email communication systems 14–15; information communication technology 13
Communication Decency Act 65
The Compendium of United Nations Standards and Norms in Crime Prevention and Criminal Justice 58
Computer Misuse Act, 1990 (CMA) 18, 32n32, 32n33, 33n34, 76
computer technology 15
Convention against Torture and Other Cruel, Inhuman or Degrading Treatment or Punishment 59
Convention on Cybercrime (2001) 36, 43
Convention on the Rights of the Child 59
copyright and trademark-related offences 77
copyright violation 21
correctional administration 74
Council of Europe Convention on the Prevention of Terrorism, 2005 14, 61
Council of Europe Convention on the Protection of Children against Sexual Exploitation and Sexual Abuse (Lanzarote Convention, 2007) 14, 61

100 Index

counter bullying 39
COVID-19 pandemic 5, 13, 19, 23, 25, 27
crime-on-crime victims 58
criminal justice machinery 6; victim assistance from 66–68
cyberattacks 62
cyberbullying 22, 38
cyber bystanders 52
Cyber Civil Rights Initiative 63
Cybercrime Prevention Act of 2012 68
cyber-crimes 5
cyber-crimes, policing new patterns of 47; and behaviour of the victims 48–52
cyber-crime victimisation 51, 57, 73; criminal justice machinery, victim assistance from 66–68; intermediaries, victim assistance from 64–66; international instruments for victim assistance 57–63; non-governmental stakeholders, victim assistance from 63–64; by way of infringement of intellectual properties 21–22
cyber-crime victimisation, general patterns of 13, 14; child online sexual exploitation 25; cyber espionage 19–21; cyberstalking 24; cyberterrorism 14–16; cyberwarfare and attack on government data 16; financial frauds and hacking 23–24; hate and misogynist speech on cyberspace 22; illegal surveillance 24; impersonation 24; infringement of bodily privacy 25; privacy violation-related victimisation for ordinary individuals 22; profiling victims of cyber-crimes 26–28; reputation damage 26; revenge porn and non-consensual image sharing 25; unauthorised access, attack by way of 18–19; unauthorised access to computers and data 16–18
cybercriminology 5
cyber espionage 13, 19–21
cyberinfrastructure 15
cyberlaws 5
Cybersafety.org 63
cyberspace 5–6, 26, 28, 48, 94–96; hate and misogynist speech on 22
cyberspace, victims' rights in 36; freedom of speech and expression on the internet 38–40; right to be forgotten 42–43; right to be protected against online sexual offences 43–44; right to equal access to justice and fair trial 44; right to privacy 40
cyberstalking 24, 64, 80
cyberterrorism 13, 14–16, 20
cyberterrorists 16
cyberwarfare and attack on government data 16

dark net 49
dark web 94
data leaking 62
data privacy 25
data subject 37
dedicated denial of services (DDoS) 17
defence lawyers 7

defining cyber victimology 7
denial of service (DoS) 13, 17, 18
Denning, D. 15
Department of Justice 67
Deviant Place theory 5
digital devices, accessing 40
Digital Millennium Copyright Act (DMCA) 65
distributed denial of service attacks (DDoS) 13, 15, 18
document-making implement 89n40
Dussich, J. 2, 3, 4, 8; social coping theory 4

e-banking facilities 5
e-commerce 13, 23; -related frauds 26
economic crimes 13
Ecuador embassy 54
Effect Test 54
e-governance system 13, 40, 49, 94
email communication systems 14–15
entrepreneurs 26
Estonia 15
EU Convention on Cybercrime, 2001 57, 61, 81
EU General Data Protection Regulations 65, 82
European Convention on Human Rights 37
European Union Convention on Cybercrime, 2001 47, 49
European Union General Data Protection Regulations 22

Facebook 48, 66
Facebook Cambridge Analytica 41, 42, 65, 66
Fattah, E. 2, 7
female victims of cyber-crimes 28
Ferri, E. 73
financial frauds and hacking 23–24
financial institution 83n16, 86n17
Fleischer, P. 42–43
freedom of speech and expression on the internet 38–40

gaming apps 48
General Data Protection Regulation (GDPR) 36, 41, 42
genocide 39
Giftbox Exchange case (2016) 50
gift scams 23
Gohar, A. 74
Google 33n39, 42
government agencies 95
guardian-less victims 51

Hague Convention 59
Halder, D. 14
harbouring spying 76
hate and misogynist speech on cyberspace 22
Hawkins, D.J.B. 74
high-impact cyber offences 50
home-quarantined children 5
human safari 71n49
Hyok, P. J. 67

Index **101**

identification document 80
illegal surveillance 24
impersonation 24
Indian Penal Code 80, 89n37
individual victimization 67
information communication technology 13
infringement of bodily privacy 25
intellectual property rights (IPR) 6
intentional hate speech 22
intermediaries, victim assistance from 64–66
International Convention on the Elimination of All Forms of Racial Discrimination 59
International Covenant on Civil and Political Rights 59
international instruments for victim assistance 57; assistance for cyber-crime victims 61–63; UN Declarations, Principles and Guidelines Regarding Victims' Rights 58–61
international stakeholders 94
internet: companies 6; de-addiction 82; freedom of speech and expression on 38–40; right to internet access 39
Internet Corp. For Assigned Names And Numbers (ICANN) 34n65
interpersonal criminal activities 44
interpersonal online victimisation 67
Iraq 15
ISIS 15
Israel 2
Iyer, V. K. 74

Jaishankar, K. 14
Jewish synagogue 77
job scams 18, 23, 26, 51, 65, 75
Jurisdiction, Recognition & Enforcement of Judgement in Civil & Commercial Matters 54
jurisdiction as the biggest challenge for policing cyber-crimes 52–55
justice and fair trial, right to equal access to 44
juvenile offenders 51
juveniles in cyberspace 48

Kshetri, N. 14

Laden, Bin 76
Lashkar-e-Taliba 76
Laws and Customs of War on Land of 18 October 1907 (Convention IV) 59
layers of victimisation 17
legal persons 37
Lessig, L. 13, 94
Levandowsky, A. 66
Liberation Tigers of Tamil Eelam (LTTE) 14
Life Style Exposure Theory 2, 5
LinkedIn 18
Long Arm statutes 53
long-term imprisonment 77
lottery scams 23, 51

male victims of cyber-crimes 29
Manu Smriti 1
May 2012 US airstrike 76
Mendelsohn, B. 1, 7, 58
#MeToo movement 4, 39, 51
misogynist speech 22
MoMo 82
Mumbai 76

need for cyber victimology 4
NHS cyberattack case (2017) 66
NHS ransomware attack 57, 62
9/11 Twin Tower attack 6, 15, 24, 76
non-consensual image sharing 25
non-governmental stakeholders, victim assistance from 63–64
non-government organisations (NGOs) 63, 64
Nuremberg Trials of 1945–1946 2

offensive text, sending 67
Official Secrets Act, 1911 76
Onion Router Project 49
online content creators 26
online crime, victims of 39
online defamation 78
online money laundering 51
online racial abuse 22
online sexual offences, right to be protected against 43–44
online victimisation 75, 94

Penal Code 49
penology 73; critical analysis of punishments prescribed by different jurisdictions 75–81; ever-expanding dimension of 73–75; reformative and therapeutic jurisprudential approaches to 81–82
Pentagon office 15
perpetrators 24, 78, 95
personal data 37
Philippine case of the rescue of 13 women (2020) 68
phishing attacks 23
Police and Criminal Evidence Act, 1984 (PACE Act) 71n48
police training 50
policing cyber-crimes 9, 47; jurisdiction as the biggest challenge for policing cyber-crimes 52–55; policing new patterns of cyber-crimes 47–52
policing cyber victimization 67
positivist victimology 2
primary victims 2
privacy, right to 40
privacy right activists 24
privacy violation 23, 25, 26; -related victimisation for ordinary individuals 22
private data 48; price of 95
profiling victims of cyber-crimes 26–28
protected computer 17, 76, 83n4

102 Index

Protection from Harassment Act, 1997 79
Protection of Victims of International Armed Conflicts (Protocol I) of 8 June 1977 59
Protocol Additional to the Geneva Conventions of 12 August 1949 59
punishment 74

quantum of punishment 75

ransom attack 33n38, 62
reformation 74
remedial measures 78
Republic Acts of the Philippines 68
reputation damage 26
restorative justice 74
revenge porn and non-consensual image sharing 25
right to be forgotten, in cyberspace 42–43
right to be protected against online sexual offences, in cyberspace 43–44
right to equal access to justice and fair trial, in cyberspace 44
right to internet access 39
right to privacy in cyberspace 40
romance scams 23
Rome Convention, 1980 54
Rome Statute of the International Criminal Court 59, 60, 69n16, 69–70n17
Routine Activity Theory 2, 5

Schafer, S. 2
sexual harassment of women 39
sexual offences, online 43–44
Sliding Scale Approach 54
social media 95; companies 94
socio-legal infrastructure 58
speech crimes 79
spoofing 33n39
Sri Lanka 14
stakeholders 6
Stuxnet 16
Syria 15

Tallinn Manual of 2013 20
Tesla 66
therapeutic jurisprudence 74, 95
thewir terror activities 77
third-party stakeholders 49
trademark-related offences 77
Trojan attack 62

trolling 38
Trump, D. 39

unauthorised access: attack by way of 18–19; to computers 16–18
UN Declaration of Basic Principles of Justice for Victims of Crime and Abuse of Powers (1985 Declaration) 3, 57, 58, 60, 61, 63
UN Declarations, Principles and Guidelines Regarding Victims' Rights 58–61
United Nations Office on Drugs and Crime (UNODC) 49
Universal Declaration of Human Rights (UDHR) (1948) 2, 9, 37, 39
"users of cyberspace" 36
US-Israeli partnership 16

victim assistance: from criminal justice machinery 66–68; from intermediaries 64–66; from non-governmental stakeholders 63–64
victim culpability 1
victimisation 3
victim justice 95; concept of 58; programs 4
victim management 52
victimology 6, 7, 73; and its development 1–4
Victim Precipitation Theory 2, 64
victims, categorization of 1–2
video voyeurism 80, 92n41
Virtual Works Inc. v. Volkswagen of Am., Inc. 34n63
Von Hentig, H. 1, 2, 7
Voyeurism (Offences) Act 2019 80

Wall, D. 14
web companies 94
Wexler, D. B. 74
WhatsApp 67
WikiLeaks 54
Winick, B. J. 74
women, sexual harassment of 39
women bloggers 26
women YouTubers 27
Working to Halt Online Abuse (WHOA) 63
World Trade Center 15

YouTube channels 27
YouTubers 27

Zehr, H. 74
Zuckerberg, M. 66